ABOVE
THE
CIRCLE

by Marty Basch
Top of the World Communications
Intervale, New Hampshire

Above the Circle
By Marty Basch

Published by:
Top of the World Communications
PO Box 731, Intervale, NH 03845

Library of Congress Catalog Card Number: 97-90363
ISBN 0-9646510-1-7

Cover design by Peg DegliAngeli/Snow Pond
Maps by Peg DegliAngeli/Snow Pond
Cover photo by Christine Jacobs
Photos by Marty Basch

For Hannah Childs, who was a storyteller in her own right

ACKNOWLEDGMENTS

Though it may appear that a solo bicycle journey is done alone, it really isn't. There were several people back home and along the way who provided valuable assistance and information.

Both Harald Hansen of the Norwegian Tourist Board and Einar Gustavsson of the Icelandic Tourist Board endured a barrage of questions during the planning stages of this trip. They were quick with answering questions, and even had a few jokes. The two are fine ambassadors of goodwill for their countries.

Gary MacFadden, director of the Adventure Cycling Association in Missoula, Montana helped arrange for the use of some equipment. That was a big help. Both David Mark and Kevin Killourie of the Red Jersey Cyclery in Glen, New Hampshire provided their skills for the packaging of my gear to Iceland.

There were those in the journalism profession who provided outlets in newspapers, on the Internet and over the airwaves for my Arctic dispatches. Thanks go to Alan Greenwood, Mark Chapman, Jay O'Neal, Mark Guerringue, Adam Hirshan and Pat McCarthy for their encouragement. Thanks along the way go to journalists Skapti, Hanna-Lisa Skau, Steinulf Henriksen, Kari Heino and Reijo Hietala.

Also, thanks to Stein Erik Myhre in Kirkenes and Bjørn Hansen in Alta for their tips for tours. Siw Elin Wideborg was a wonderful resource in Alta too while Linda Halvorsen had patience while translating the interview with Håkon Hansen.

After the journey, time came for a book, and after reviewing the hundreds of slides taken during the trip, not one cried out to be the book's cover. So, in a last minute attempt to capture the Arctic atmosphere, management at the Mount Washington Auto Road in New Hampshire allowed me and photographer Christine Jacobs to ride up the snow-covered road to above treeline on a snowcat. This was done on Easter Sunday. The photo reflects Jacobs' excellent efforts in 40 mile per hour winds and subfreezing temperatures. Don't ask her about the ski down.

Once again, Peg DegliAngeli of Snow Pond lent her expertise for the cover design. She's a heck of a climber and cyclist too. Kevin Murphy was a big help in the cyberworld, and he gets a big thank you too. To everyone who sent me e-mail during the trip, thank you.

Thanks and hugs also go to my parents Mitch and Lynn Basch. Jan Duprey gets a special thank you because of her love and support.

Also by Marty Basch

AGAINST THE WIND

ABOVE THE CIRCLE

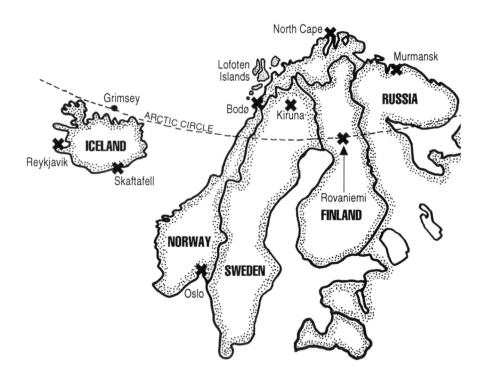

May 19- August 25, 1996

(Map not to scale)

TABLE OF CONTENTS

INTRODUCTION

I like to ride my bicycle. Plain and simple, that's why I do what I do. I'm a writer. Technology has made it so a laptop computer can fit into a pack that can be carried on a bicycle. Therefore, I ride and I write.

Once, I was contemplating riding my bicycle from Maine to Alaska. I told this to a colleague who happened to be a photographer. I said I wasn't quite sure I should do it, citing all sorts of lame reasons.

She looked at me and said: "You're a writer. It's your job."

So, I do things like this because it is my job. I'll admit it. I like this job. Actually, I love it. This isn't a job that one finds in the classified section and applies for. This is an avocation which one works for and creates. Not many people are going to be at their job one day when the boss comes over, taps you on the shoulder and asks if you want to spend the summer biking in some remote section of the world.

I used to be a journalist who ran after the news. I tried it for several years and found I didn't like it that much. I liked interviewing people who were fun and had interesting lives. I liked finding new places, at least new to me, and writing about them. I found I enjoyed writing about the thoughts I had while trying sports like skiing, snowboarding, snowshoeing, hiking and biking. I liked the people I found too.

So that is all I am trying to do. Find people, places and things and write about them. I just happen to be on a bicycle while I'm doing it. That's it.

I have been fortunate. In a sense, I don't have many needs that tie a person down. I don't have a high comfort level. I tend to be happy with the simple things.

Now, the simple can be complex. Namely, I mean the computer. I don't know much about them. I can't tell a megabyte from a kilowatt. I don't care much how they work. I just want them to work when I need them to work.

I first carried a computer during a Maine to Alaska ride in 1994 which I wrote about in *Against the Wind*. Though people were amazed that a bicyclist would carry a computer, hooking up to a commercial online service to e-mail columns back to newspapers was fairly easy.

It was easy in Iceland, Norway, Finland and Sweden too. The computer was placed in a soft case and deposited in a waterproof kayaker's bag. This all fit in one rear saddlebag.

Now I wasn't quite sure that it would be so easy in Scandinavia to go online. I worried. I don't like to worry. I thought maybe the phone lines would be different. I thought maybe this difference (real or imaginary) would mean the computer would blow up when I tried to go online. It didn't.

A commercial online computer service had phone numbers in each country I traveled. I dialed the numbers and was online. There weren't any problems except for the one time I typed in the wrong phone number and it didn't work. I found businesses geared toward tourism most helpful in gaining telephone access. Places like visitor information offices would let me use their phones. Sometimes people who put me up for the night would let me use their phone lines. Newspaper offices were a good place. Once, I went into a telephone store in Sweden and they let me hook up for free.

I also worried about electricity. I thought maybe I would plug the computer into the outlet and it would blow up because the current was different. It didn't. I bought adapters before I left for Europe so I could plug the computer into the different outlets. They worked.

During my trip, I would sometimes seek out the media to do stories about me. I wanted to see if anyone would contact me in cyberspace during this adventure. They did. One article even resulted in an invitation to the northernmost town in the world. The media would also print the Internet site where my columns would be published. This would enable people in Scandinavia to tap into the Internet and follow stories published in a New Hampshire newspaper.

I am not a sponsored rider. The money for these trips come out of my pocket. However, I do get paid for the work I do along the way. Weekly columns appeared in *The Conway Daily Sun* in New Hampshire and on their Internet site. I had a few pieces in *The Boston Herald* and the *Nashua (NH) Telegraph* too. Twice a month I had stories on the New England Sports Network's SportsCircuit site.

For fun, a deal was worked out with New Hampshire Public Radio. I was to call them collect and we would talk about my trip twice a month. The only drawback was that the station couldn't accept collect phone calls. I didn't learn this until I tried to call them collect from Iceland. I put the calls on my phone credit card. I was reimbursed.

A lot of people wonder how I train for these trips. Well, I ride my bicycle. I'm fairly active. I stay in reasonable condition, whatever that may be. I don't ride much in the winter, instead going skiing, snowboarding and snowshoeing. I like to hike also. But I've been going on long-distance bike trips for over 20 years. I know I'll get stronger as I click off the miles. Plus, a little pain makes for great copy.

Life goes on. I intend to keep riding and writing as long as I can, as long as it stays interesting and as long as I am healthy.

I'm not the only one doing it. There are others. There will be more. Ride on.

ABOVE
THE
CIRCLE

CHAPTER ONE

Vasta Matter

What do you say to a naked man who is hitting you on the back with a bunch of birch leaves? The inclination might be to ask the guy to quit. But the truth be told, I didn't want him to stop. I was enjoying this. Each swipe of the bouquet on my solid flesh unloosed the sweet, aromatic essence from within the birch leaves. My skin would sting as the birch twigs beat against my neck too. The leaves became wet. Some would leave the bunch and stick right to my back.

The fragrance was even more pronounced because it was damn hot. Hot is good in Finland. When it's hot, even during those rare days in summer, it means you are taking part in a Finnish tradition — the sauna. Not only was the 71-year-old man naked, so was I. Perspiration came out to drip down on to the wooden benches in the wood-fired sauna. Flesh glistened in the murky room. The only sounds came from the swoosh of the *vasta* hitting my back and neck and the hissing of the steam as Pentti Vaarama would dip a ladle into a bucket of cold water and drip the water onto the devilishly hot stones. The steam coils around you and slams into your body with the force of a tidal wave. The rush can be overwhelming. Yet in the end, it is there to loosen the tightness caused by a long day of bicycle riding.

The sauna is a Scandinavian ritual. The Finns think nothing of having a few beers, getting naked and heading into the sweat box. It seems that every house, or apartment in the country has a sauna. I once read somewhere that there were more saunas than cars in Finland and that there was one sauna for every four people.

So it should have been no surprise when Pentti invited me into his sauna. It's just a display of northern hospitality. The sauna, pronounced sow-na (like a little piggy), was just outside the summer house he shared with his wife Terttu, about thirty miles south of the Arctic Circle near the city of Rovaniemi.

It was here the two would tend to their love of the outdoors and grow plenty of onions, lettuce and strawberries during the never-ending summer days, the midnight sun ensuring quick growth during the oh-so-short season. They had a greenhouse to grow tomatoes. Their five acres in the woods, it was said, contained 6,500 pine trees.

I knew all this, not because of Pentti and Terttu, but because of one of their daughters, Hannele Vaarama, and her husband, Kai Leinonen. Pentti and Terttu spoke no English. Well, not exactly no English. They spoke better English than I did Finnish and I didn't speak any Finnish. Well, not exactly no Finnish. I had been in the country for a few days and could say one word, *kiitos*, which meant thank you. Thank you doesn't get you very far in a conversation. However, if you only know one word in a language, it's a good one to know. *Kiitos* and a smile could do wonders in Finland, like *tak* and a smile would do in Iceland, Norway and Sweden.

Hannele and Kai spoke English, and spoke it very well. Actually, it was their idea to visit her parents. Pentti and Terttu had never met an American bicycling around the Arctic Circle before. I had never been hit in the back by a naked man with a bunch of birch branches. So it seemed like a good thing for all the parties involved.

Kai and Hannele hadn't met too many Americans biking around near the top of Europe either. I was the first one. They were the first Finns I had met vacationing in Norway just one month before. You know how it is when you are traveling by bicycle. You come across people you like. You exchange addresses and part with words like, "If you are ever in the area, you can stay with us." Guess what? I was one ocean away from home, on the other side of the Atlantic and I was going to make it a point to pedal down to Rovaniemi, Finland, about five miles south of the Arctic Circle, and take them up on their offer. I liked them. They spoke English. They offered me a free place to stay. They said if I visited them they would give me a "good sauna." You couldn't ask for more.

That's how I ended up naked in the sauna on a July night with Pentti. By this time though, I was almost a sauna-taking veteran. This was my second experience. The first had been a few days before at Kai and Hannale's house. Just like you offer a guest something to eat or drink, the couple offered me a sauna. I accepted.

This first session was a solo experience. The sauna was located off the kitchen through a door which also housed the washing and drying machines. Outside the sauna was a shower.

The idea is to enter the sauna still wet after cleaning yourself. Once inside as the mercury soars to the 150 degree (Fahrenheit) mark and beyond, you sit back and relax, letting the heat infiltrate your body and open the skin's pores. After a few minutes, leave the sauna, shower and head back inside. This can be done several times.

The ritual can seem a bit tedious to those who have never done it before. But I had a *vasta* which Hannale had prepared. The birch switches are wrapped with a twig and hung upside down to dry. Hannale gave me the *vasta* before I stepped into the sauna and told me how to use it.

I took the bouquet into the sauna and put it down by my side, letting the heat soak through everything. There was silence. I looked down at the *vasta*, wondering if using it meant I was a perverse individual who would go blind after a self-flagellation session. Besides, no one would have to know. I wouldn't have to tell anyone about this.

I leaned over and grasped the *vasta*. Like Hannale instructed, I dipped the bouquet into a bucket of water in the sauna.

Then I beat myself.

Using my right hand, I took the *vasta* over my head and beat to the left. Then I would lean to the left and start beating the right side of my back. The leaves crashed against my back. The scent was released. I was having a good time.

My right hand was tired. I switched the *vasta* and started the same process with my weaker hand. The sauna filled with the rustling of leaves. I beat myself some more.

I left the sauna with a smile.

Hannale and Kai didn't even need to ask if I liked it. My smile said a lot.

So when Pentti asked if I wanted to take a sauna at his place, I was quick to answer in the affirmative.

This sauna differed from the one in Hannale's house in two ways. First, this one was wood-fired. The first sauna had been electric. Finnish sauna connoisseurs insist an electric sauna is not an authentic experience. They might say the heat is dry, especially compared to the steam from a wood-fired stove. To me, heat is heat.

The second difference was not as subtle.

This time, I wouldn't be alone. It was explained to me that Pentti would join me to ensure my trip to the sauna would be done properly.

What is a guest to do? One must never insult the host. When in Finland, one must do as the Finns do.

3

We headed to the sauna and my date with a moment of naked truth. The sauna was cooking. Pentti checked the fire and the placement of the water buckets. When two people don't share a common language, a lot of emphasis is placed on hand motion. Pentti disrobed and then indicated I should do the same.

Vanity? Modesty? Self-consciousness? What is it about getting naked in the presence of a total stranger that caused me to think about wearing a towel, and just a towel, into the sauna. What's the big deal? Who cares who's got what or who doesn't have what? Birth mark? Beer gut? So what.

Off came the clothes.

I stepped into the sauna with only a nervous smile.

Pentti and I rinsed in the buckets of water. Then we sat in the quiet. On occasion he would ladle water onto the rocks and steam would rise and spread. We tried to communicate. This was terribly frustrating. Through Kai and Hannale I had learned a lot about Pentti and Terttu. Pentti had written a book about handwriting analysis. The two had lived through the agony of World War II. They had many stories to tell and because of the few words we had between us, we ended up sitting in the steam in silence.

The silence was broken when Pentti beat me with the vasta. He didn't even ask if I wanted to be hit with the *vasta*. He just picked it up and continued the tradition.

Not long after that, we left the sauna. Had it been winter, we would have rolled in the snow to cool down. Some sauna seekers rush down to a nearby lake or stream for a zippy dip. Even in winter, Finns are known to cut a hole in a frozen lake and jump in.

This was summer. There wasn't a shower in this sauna. Instead, we just rinsed ourselves off with the buckets of water and repeated the process.

Still naked, we walked outside into daylight to a room next door where a fire was blazing in the hearth. I put on a borrowed robe and sat down in front of the fire with Pentti.

The only sounds were the crackling fire.

Pentti stood up and took an imaginary *vasta* in his hand and started to make the motion of hitting himself on the back with it.

He looked over at me and mustered together a few words of English.

"We in Finland big masochists," he said with a laugh.

I joined in with my own laughter. The laughter came from deep within. The laughter was pure joy, joy in a realization that getting naked in a sauna is a damn good thing. It's not about nudity. It's about enjoyment. It's about relaxing. It's about sharing a way of life, a culture. It's about touching the spirit and strengthening the body.

That's why I do this, I thought. That's why I get on my bicycle and go for a ride for a few months. It's to soak up the atmosphere, see the sunset from a new perspective, wonder where the stars go in summer, meet the people, and, even if it's necessary, get naked with them in their very own home.

The Arctic Circle conjures up images of Eskimos, polar bears and igloos. Though these all exist, they are not just what the Far North is about. Nor are all of these things found in all places in the Arctic. For a while, I thought the Arctic was about bikini-clad Norsewomen. That's because I saw one in a brochure about travel to the top of Europe. Also in the brochure were laudatory ramblings about adventure, reindeer, over-sized trout and wild berries like gold called cloudberries.

One slick glossy travel planner talked about northern Norway this way: "This region, atop of the world, is known as the 'Land of the Midnight Sun.' Here midnight might be mistaken for midday during the summer, adding even more daylight hours to enjoy a wild and beautiful countryside. In the north, Norway becomes a land of craggy cliffs that abut the sea, deep fertile valleys, forgotten moors, islands where life has remained unchanged for generations, and cities and towns where hearty people are eager to show visitors the ways of life above the Arctic Circle."

Now wait a minute. We're talking about the Arctic here. It's supposed to be a barren, frigid, isolated place with tundra as far as the eye can see. This is supposed to be a place where the natives hunt with spears, gnaw whale blubber and anyone who owns a refrigerator might also be interested in purchasing a bridge in Brooklyn. This is no man's land. It is a frozen desert, wasteland.

There's much more to it.

It's also a place with shopping malls, multi-story buildings and public transportation systems. It's a place with a city with nearly 500,000 residents. The Arctic is a place with universities, sporting events, warm-hearted people and even fast food restaurants.

The Arctic is a place with life.

And when there is life and relative warmth, there is room for bicycle travel.

My fascination with the north has been lifelong. There is beauty in freshly fallen snow, the sparkling morning frost and the calm of a trackless frozen lake. The winter has its own toys. Skiers, snowshoers, snowboarders, sledders, ice climbers, skaters and mushers all play in their version of paradise. Bicycle travel is also possible during this time. Those who realize you can ride in the same clothing in which you cross-country ski are still out on the roads and trails.

It's not the optimal time to ride, but there are those who enjoy it. So when the snow melts and the sun shines intermittently, a new season awakens the north and it is then I like to explore it from the seat of a bicycle.

The idea of seeing the Arctic by bicycle may seem an implausible venture, foolish and even idiotic. It is not. Spin a globe. There are roads that cross the circle at 66 degrees, 30 minutes — the general accepted median for the forever shifting boundary — all over the world.

Look at the globe from a polar view. If Antarctica is in your face, turn the globe upside down. Now you are looking at the top of the world.

Take your index finger and follow the perforated line. That is the Arctic Circle. The line is not cold to the touch. Well, unless you've kept the globe in the freezer. The line hits eight countries — the United States, Canada, Greenland, Iceland, Norway, Sweden, Finland and Russia.

Alaska is in the United States. The Dalton Highway is in Alaska and it cuts up 415 miles from Fairbanks to Prudhoe Bay and the Arctic Ocean. Bikers looking to ride Alaska to Argentina, tip to tale, often dip their wheels in the chilling waters. The road follows the Alaska Pipeline which transports oil from way up there to everywhere else. I've met a couple of bikers who have ridden this road. They say there isn't much once you are out of the Fairbanks area. When a biker says there isn't much, you've got to believe it. They know the difference between something and nothing much better than a motorist who only has to depress the accelerator a little more to get from nowhere to somewhere. So, if there is nothing there, why go? To say you've done it? Personal accomplishment? For some, these are valid reasons.

Not me. I wanted to explore. I wanted to take my time to see, feel, hear and taste life in an Arctic summer.

My search continued.

Next door is Canada and the rugged Yukon. The Dempster Highway begins east of Dawson City, crosses the Continental Divide a few times and then cuts into the Northwest Territories to Fort McPherson and the end of the road in Inuvik. That's the summer end of the road. In winter, the road extends on frozen waterways to Tuktoyaktuk. The road is only about 450 miles. I'm inclined to do that trip one day. I've seen pictures of a man dressed in a tuxedo who greets visitors at the Arctic Circle. I'd like to meet him. I'd be interested in knowing where he goes on a coffee break. There's not much shown on a map. Then again, there's probably a visitor center with rest rooms and knickknacks nearby.

With America and Canada not having too many miles of rider-friendly roads above the circle, I started to look elsewhere.

Next stop on the index finger tour is Greenland. Greenland should be named Iceland. There is more ice there than green. The Arctic Circle pierces through the heart of Greenland. On a map, there appears to be a lot of places to ride. There is one drawback though. The island is covered by lots of snow year-round. That doesn't mean someone can't ride a bicycle around it. It just means that that someone wasn't going to be me.

Take the finger and make sure it doesn't sink as you cross the Denmark Strait and come ashore in Iceland. Iceland should be named Greenland. There is green there, and ice too. From a marketing perspective though, the country should have a referendum and change it. They would get more fair-weather tourists. People tend to get turned off by a vacation that implies ice.

The island nation is just below the circle. That makes it sub-Arctic. But wait a minute. There's a tiny dot off the northern coast of Iceland. That little, bitty speck of land is an island that is part of Iceland. It straddles the Arctic Circle. So, that part of Iceland is Arctic. The island is called Grimsey and is reachable via ferry from the second largest city in Iceland called Akureyri.

A handful of hardy souls live, fish and play lots of chess to pass the time on Grimsey. Word is, there were times the game was taken so seriously that those who lost important contests flung themselves off the craggy cliffs to their death in the frigid North Atlantic. Guess that happened in the days before cable television.

Iceland doesn't look like a bad place to ride either. It's virtually round. There is a road that encircles the entire country called the Ring Road. Iceland looked like a possibility.

So did Norway. Cross the Norwegian Sea by plane or boat and there you are in a long, narrow country that oddly enough looks like a crooked index finger. The circle slices through Norway at a point which leaves hundreds of miles of road above it. The road happens to lead to the northernmost point on mainland Europe reachable by public road — North Cape. The thought of being the northernmost thing in Europe for a moment on a given day made me giddy. I could stand there on the edge of the world, hold an imaginary American flag, peer over, look down into the abyss and hope I didn't have a vertigo attack. Yes, there appeared to be a lot of places to be explored in the nation by the sea. Norway borders both Sweden and Finland. Guess what? The dotted line ran through those two Scandinavian countries too. Now four countries were looking good.

Finland borders Russia. The index finger stopped at the border and took a look around Russia's Kola Peninsula. It continued. The finger crossed into Siberia. The finger sent an S.O.S. signal to the brain rather quickly. It went something like, "What are you? Nuts?"

Bad enough I didn't speak Icelandic, Norwegian, Finnish or Swedish. I didn't speak Russian either. I couldn't read Russian. I didn't know the Russian alphabet. Nor could I read the other languages, but at least the majority of their letters are the same as English.

But that wasn't the real issue. The thought of crossing into Russia by myself didn't feel right. Scandinavian images played in my mind's cinema. I would meet a blonde named Inga and her twin sister Helga. They would befriend me and we would live happily ever after near the top of the world. We would cross-country ski through the mountains and by the fjords and if I fell and broke my leg, well, no problem. There's socialized medicine. I wouldn't have to worry about getting killed because murder rates were low. We could live on the pickled herring and vast quantities of vodka. Soon, I would learn their language and converse in its sing-song lilt. I would change my name to Thor.

Then the mind's projector played other images, those of Russia. Pictures of long bread lines, old ladies in kerchiefs, borscht, and rows upon rows of soldiers and tanks crossed the screen. Bad movies about Russian spies and the Cold War took center stage. A short advertisement for Russian vodka and caviar held my interest for a moment, but soon 30-plus years of memories laced with propaganda flooded through me. Instead of Helga and Inga, I saw Natasha and Boris. Natasha would be a spy. She would invite me to her lair. I would be weak and succumb to her KGB tactics, spilling my guts about American secrets I knew nothing about. Natasha would record the conversation. I would be found guilty in a speedy trial and sent to the *gulag*. I would never be heard from again, the focus of my life becoming a mean, huge, ugly, bald guard named Ivan who had a thing for foreigners.

Did I want to go to Russia by myself? I could answer that in a word. *Nyet.*

My finger soon reached a familiar place again — Alaska. A plan started to materialize. I could cycle Iceland's Ring Road and take the boat to Grimsey. Following the Icelandic loop, I could fly to Scandinavia and make my way to the Arctic Circle and ride another loop through Norway, Sweden and Finland. Thus, my trip would be near and above the Arctic Circle.

Now I needed information.

If there is a guide book to bicycling near and above the Arctic Circle, I couldn't find it. There are plenty of guide books which provide a flavor for what was to come. The tourist boards of the countries provided free and colorful brochures. The Internet had information. Maps were easy to find through a mail-order house. Who cares if a few were in German? And Norwegian. And Swedish. And English. A place is a place by any name.

Then again, I'm not the kind of traveler who needs to know what is around every bend. I like mystery and excitement in my travels. Believe me, if there is a major hill to be climbed, the locals will tell you about it. If there is a major site to be seen, the locals will point you there. One of the most satisfying parts of travel is discovery. Sure, tons of people might have seen what you have found, but the point is you found it. Whether it be a swimming hole found or a gas station attendant who lets you camp in the back of the station, this is where the essence of travel lives. Travelers discover. Tourists follow.

I was not concerned about language. English is probably America's number one export. Through television programs and rock songs on the radio, the youth of Europe have an idea of how to speak English. Starting before they are in double digits, many students are taught English in school. As a rule with a lot of holes in it, people born before World War II would speak German as a second language. Those conceived after the war, have a tendency to know English. Plus, outside of America, people tend to know more than one language.

I wasn't concerned about food. Leave the McFood at home. I didn't want to see any familiar fast food signs. I eat too much McFood as it is. I didn't need it on the road, especially at prices which would leave me laughing. I wanted to sample the local fare. If they ate raw fish, dish it up. If they ate reindeer, let's chow down on a Rudolph burger. If they put cheese in their coffee, let's take a few swigs and hold the mayo.

I wasn't concerned about my safety in the Scandinavian countries. I didn't care if the prices were astronomical. I would find the most economical way of eating. I wouldn't worry about expensive accommodations. Money for youth hostels and guest houses would be budgeted but Scandinavia is home to a practice which translates into "Everyman's Right." Iceland, Norway, Sweden and Finland observe a law which allows camping virtually anywhere on public land, so long as you are at least 150 yards from a house and leave no trace. I would employ this right every chance I got.

I did have a concern about the weather, though. The summer is short in the Far North. Broadly speaking, summer can start July 1 and end by mid-August. That's the summer with black flies, mosquitoes and temperatures that hit 70. That summer does exist in the Arctic. I was concerned about the weather prior to it, the spring. Spring can be a pseudonym for winter in those parts. Snow, temperatures near freezing and days of rain are a part of spring, as are days of sunshine and temperatures in the 60s. It was the snow and cold that bothered me. I had figured the trip would be about 3,000 miles. The idea wasn't to set a land speed record. I would take my time. Smell the roses. I needed three months for this. I had to fit my trip in between the snow.

There is no weather guarantee in this part of the world during summer. Snow can fall at any time. The temperatures can dip. The rains can soak you. I decided to head to Iceland first, mainly because it was closest and most south. The Icelandic Tourist Board encouraged me to go as close to June as I possibly could, actually suggesting I go in July when the weather is better. In May, when I wanted to go, the weather would be precarious and some of the visitor services (campgrounds, stores, information booths) wouldn't be operating yet.

I decided on May 19.

There was one other concern — Russia. The more I looked at the maps near the top of Europe, the more I looked into the eyes of the bear. Russia was so close to Norway. It was so close to Finland. How could I not go?

My curiosity was peaked. I found an old World Book encyclopedia with a map of Scandinavia and Russia. It showed an area called the Kola Peninsula with a city named Murmansk. There appeared to be a road that went from the Norwegian border at Kirkenes to Murmansk, the largest city in the world above the Arctic Circle, and then down to a place on the Russian-Finnish border named Raja-Jooseppi. This could be part of an Arctic Loop.

Could I go to Russia? Better yet, did I really want to go? Again, that voice from somewhere inside me asked the question, how could I not go?

Perhaps the call to the Russian Tourist Board in New York was an omen. "You want to go to Murmansk," inquired the accented voice on the other end of the phone. "Why?" The voice suggested Moscow or St. Petersburg, both below the circle. Murmansk wasn't written up in slick brochures. There wasn't much available in the guide books. When I asked to be sent a map, the voice told me to find one on the Internet.

I did learn that I needed a visa to visit Russia. Usually the visa business is taken care of by a tour operator. I was going solo, so I was the tour operator.

"Okay, so what do I do?," I asked.

"You must get invitation," said the voice.

"From who?"

"From tourist organization in Russia."

Silence.

"Let me get this straight. I need a letter from someone in Russia to invite me to Russia?," I asked.

"Yes."

"But I don't know anyone."

"You might try sports club."

"I don't know a sports club."

"You can find one in Moscow."

"Okay, let's say I find a sports club in Moscow. Then what?," I asked.

"They write a letter for you and you get a visa."

"Why would they write a letter for me if they don't know me?," I asked.

"This is how it is done," he said.

"Why can't you invite me?," I asked.

"I don't know you," he said.

"Neither does the sports club," I replied.

The conversation went on for a few more minutes. I felt like I was on a treadmill, going nowhere in the dance of bureaucracy. Round and round we danced, until finally, the voice came up with the name of a company in Moscow that organizes bike tours.

I figured I would give them a shot.

So I faxed them my plans which basically consisted of saying I think I want to scoot into Russia for a few days, somewhere near Murmansk. Can you invite me?.

They faxed me back within 48 hours.

They would gladly write me a letter, but it would cost me. "Visa support costs 50 USD" it read. The letter detailed how I should wire the money to a bank in New York. "To support visa we are to know your date of birth and passport number. Please also advise the duration of the trip (exact dates) and destinations."

Ah, the bureaucracy spawns a cottage industry.

The bureaucracy also spawned a problem. Not only didn't I know exactly where I was going, I didn't know exactly when either. Spontaneity was key. I didn't want to be locked into any dates.

I faxed them back, trying to explain this.

They faxed me back and wrote: "We can support your visa to Russia for two months. Please indicate the exact place of crossing Russian border and the date of entering Russia. In this case your visa will last two months.... Please note, the most convenient way to enter Russia from Finland is Vyborg (close to St. Petersburg)."

I went to look at a map. Vyborg was a long way south of the Arctic Circle. This was not even close to where I wanted to exit Russia. We needed a translator here.

So, I faxed them back, explaining that I probably would cross into

11

Russia from Kirkenes and cross back at Raja-Jooseppi. I wanted to stay above the Arctic Circle. I gave them a date of July 1 to cross into Russia, knowing that I would get a two month visa. I could go into Russia any time after July 1, wrapping things up by the end of August. That seemed reasonable.

I wired the bank the $50.

I faxed them the fact that I sent the bank the money.

They faxed me back. Keep in mind, we are now two weeks into international faxing. The letter told me to apply for a visa with the Russian consulate in New York. The visa would be for Borisoglebsk (Kirkenes), Murmansk, Nikel, Kandalaksha, Vjaltilja and Vyborg.

The letter informed me that "only Finnish citizens can cross the border at Raja-Jooseppi. The border in this point is free for them and closed for other people."

Great, for fifty bucks I check in any time I wanted, but I could never leave. This meant I could cross in where I wanted in Norway, but had to go way out of my way to complete the loop in Finland.

This didn't sit well with me. But I didn't push it. I figured at worst, I could pop in for a day, say hi, try the borscht, drink vodka and leave.

I sent in my application, visa support letter and photos to the Russian consulate, along with the processing fee of $40.

Three weeks later, I had my Russian visa.

During this comedy, I had searched the Internet for people who had traveled to Russia's Kola Peninsula. I struck gold in the form of a British journalist who had spent 10 years there. We entered into an e-mail relationship for a few weeks prior to my leaving and answered quite a few questions. I saved some of our letters and condensed them. I learned:

1. "There is no concept of a tourist office in Murmansk which is sad since the Kola is a fantastic travel destination. I am not sure that you will have that much joy with bicycles since the larger highways are functional straight strips of tarmac with nothing but forest on either side and the smaller highways are always difficult if you get caught on them without permission. My advice is go for it anyway and if the Army stops you don't give them any money! Maps are actually not too bad nowadays and they are almost free (a few rubles) if you buy them in Murmansk.

2. Places that I would recommend visiting are Severomorsk (home of the Northern fleet), Monchegorsk (to see what pollution can do to a pristine wilderness), Verkny Tuloma (rustic Russian village on the Tuloma river), and Lovozero (the Sami capital of Kola).

3. The Norwegian and Finnish sides are very, very well served by tourist information and facilities. In Norway the choice of idyllic places is almost endless.

4. The best way to cycle through Kola is to cross the border at Kirkenes and cycle along the coastal highway to Murmansk. The east of Kola is hopeless for bikes; no roads at all.

5. If you cannot speak Russian then have an official looking letter — one from the Cycle club in Moscow would be good. Try and learn some cheerful Russian words and say them with a smile. In the Arctic a smile goes a long way.

6. There are a few roads east of Murmansk but only for twenty km's or so, then they peter out. Remember the Soviet Union reconstructed the northern part of the Kola as the largest military base in the world — much of the peninsula was high-security and lack of roads contributed to that deliberate isolation.

7. Murmansk is the second largest port in Russia after Vladivostock. It is a hopelessly ugly city and rather melancholy at the moment. Most of the men are fishermen or sailors. They have an excellent museum, growing cultural scene and decent shopping (food is not cheap but it is good and plentiful). It is also home to the Murmansk Shipping Company which handles all the shipping through the Arctic.

8. Camp where you like out in the forests. If you are close to a village ask permission of one of the village elders (find some children, they'll be able to muster enough English to assist you)."

The journalist went even further. He provided me with phone numbers and addresses of English-speaking friends of his in Murmansk that included a boat captain, English translator and teacher.

While I was getting support from an Internet stranger, the media was filled with news of the upcoming Russian elections. In 1996, the Communists had a shot at winning. Family and friends didn't want me to go. The horror stories started to come. Someone had a friend who had a friend who was detained in Russia for no reason. Somebody knew someone who had his money stolen. And on and on the stories went.

All I knew, is that when the day came for me to cross into Russia, I would make my decision then.

So armed with the right clothing, equipment, money, paperwork, and a taste for adventure, I was ready for my Arctic ride.

CHAPTER TWO

Ride On

Within minutes, the clean and polite city of Reykjavik was no more. Some 270,000 people live in Iceland and about half of them or so call the metropolis home. The city was neat. Tiny lawns, so rare on the rest of the Iceland nation, were green in spring. How Icelanders love their flowers. Even in mid-May, they dotted the urban landscape and apartment houses to give bursts of color against a cellophane-gray sky that only rarely allows the sun to shine all day.

But head south from Reykjavik and soon, all of that changes. The green is no more and a wild, rocky character is the norm. For the next 21 days or so, my trail will be the Ring Road, a two-lane country road that encircles this island in the Far North.

The higher one cycles over the many hills, the closer the snow becomes. I've yet to touch it, but I will. Or perhaps, it will fall down from the sky and touch me. Ahead, so far ahead it seemed, the snow waited. So did the ice. Eleven percent of Iceland's land mass is a glacier, the largest one in all of Europe. My route would skirt it and fill my horizon for days. Mark Twain would be very well prepared for an Icelandic spring. If you don't like the weather, just wait a minute, he had once advised his fellow Americans. This applies in Iceland too. Perhaps it can be modified to if you don't like the weather, just wait a second. It was only my first day out and already, the mercury was dropping as I left the city. Dark mountains and soft moss accounted for much of the scenery.

14

I know that scenery will not remain the same in this land of seemingly impossible juxtapositions of contrasts. The first look out from the airplane's window upon approach will tell you that immediately. The land takes on a lunar quality. I will never get to the moon. I will never get to Mars. But I have been to Iceland. It is as close to the heavens as most of us will ever get. American astronauts have trained for missions to the moon in the country's desolate interior where many Icelandic heroes and villains of yesterday are said to have done battle or hid among the isolation of the mountains, deserts and waterfalls.

First glimpses from the plane and from the airport in Keflavik make visitors think Iceland is a lunar landscape of lava. Hardly a tree, the homes were clustered by the frigid Atlantic shores, hugging each other like humans do for warmth. This can be a brutally cold place.

First impressions and a myriad of other thoughts jumbled through my head as I set the pedals in motion on the morning of May 21 in Reykjavik. Jet lag, time changes, new foods, exhaustion and excitement can screw up anyone's world and I was no exception.

What could have been the longest day in my life started two days earlier in a small New Hampshire town. It was a never-ending, last minute whirlwind of supplies bought, equipment checked, luggage packed, bike boxed, good-byes and tears shed to loved ones. The three hour car drive to Boston's Logan Airport was filled with even more excitement and tension as the reality of a new journey started to take shape in the form of a steadily approaching departure time for a red-eye flight.

Sleep did not come easily, if at all, on the flight. The movie passed time, as did conversation with fellow passengers who were using the Icelandic stop as a gateway to other points in Europe. Adrenaline made me turn down the dinner and even the complimentary wine. Soon enough, it was morning in Iceland, though my internal clock had a hard time believing it wasn't still the middle of the night.

Of course, the view from the plane's window was a signal you weren't in Kansas anymore. Sure, the airline attendants made announcements in English and Icelandic. But it wasn't until I was whisked quickly through passport control by an officer with only mild interest in my travel plans and a stamp placed in my passport did it hit me. I was up there, just below the circle.

English faded and was replaced by a white noise I was to hear for the next three months — the chatter of a language I didn't understand. The currencies would be different. The foods would be different. The customs would be different. And what English I came across would be English with an accent. English with syntax out of whack. English with missing verbs. English that made me pay attention.

Adrenaline was the life force that continued to move me as I boarded a bus to Reykjavik with my boxed bike and body bag. The body bag wasn't one that actually contained a corpse. It was the name I tagged it as it inched near me on the luggage belt. The oversized duffle bag contained all my gear. When it made its approach on the belt, it looked like a big, fat stiff. Weighed like a stiff too.

One person with a boxed bike, body bag and jet lag can be a comedy show. Even with the assistance of a luggage cart, maneuvering something that is too fat, too long and too bulky through an airport makes you appear inept and just plain stupid. I was all too glad to have everything under the bus, in the proper place, for the ride into the city.

The ride gave me time to scan the Icelandic moonscape. But within minutes, the bus made its final stop at a downtown hotel and it was there, still sleepless, I had the task of putting together the bike in the box.

I quivered.

I have admitted it in the past, and I will admit it again. I am mechanically-challenged. That said, I have never let it interfere with a long distance bicycle trip where I might one day be miles from nowhere, with no one around and I will have to totally rely on my ineptitude to fix something I have no idea how. That supposes I can actually identify the problem. Duct tape can only get you so far.

The guys back at the Red Jersey Cyclery in Glen, New Hampshire knew this. They knew they were dealing with a mechanical idiot who could usually fix a flat tire, and had enough common sense to bring his bike in for a tune up every 1,000 miles or so. So they tried to package the bike in the most user-friendly way as to prevent me from giving up starting my trip before it even began.

They were successful.

Bicycles don't come assembled straight out of the box. Unfortunately, you must put them together, and use tools. Tools are not my friend. I have tried to avoid tools in my life. Instead, I am of the ilk, that if something needs repair, you call the friend who has tools and promise him copious amounts of beer in exchange for his labor. During the course of his labor, you can offer assistance by actually handing him the tool he requires, or pop the cap off the beer bottle and put it firmly into his hand so as not to disturb him as he twists something with a tool. I still cringe if I have to go into a hardware store, even if it is just to buy more duct tape. Without duct tape, I would fall apart.

However, growing older in life means you recognize your strengths and weaknesses. I know I can't go through life entirely without tools. So I carry them. At times, I even use them. First, I search very diligently for someone who knows what to do with them. If that person can't be found,

I try to use them.

So it was, I began to remove the contents of the bike box in the back of a hotel, right next to a dumpster. The frame was intact. Both wheels had been removed. An axle had been taken out of the rear wheel. The seat had been taken out from the frame. The front handlebar had been twisted to the side and removed as to fit inside the box. The front and rear racks had been taken off. The pedals were off.

Now I had to put the jigsaw puzzle back together. I used two allen wrenches. Actually figured out the right ones. Used a wrench too. I wish I had stopped someone to take a picture of this sight.

The seat and post fit right where it was supposed to. The front wheel went right between the fork. The axle slipped into its hole and the rear wheel went on. "Righty tighty, lefty loosey," chimed in my head as the pedals were screwed back into place.

The handlebar stem slipped into place. The stem was tightened. The brakes actually worked too! So did the gears!

The rear rack was next on the agenda. With only an allen wrench, the screws fit quickly and snugly into their places. The front rack loomed. This would be the toughest challenge as I would have to negotiate the placing of four screws and four clamps with only two tools and two hands. Surprisingly, even this was accomplished with little profanity as the ace bike mechanics had left the clamps on the fork and all I had to do was remove the screws, insert the rack and slip the screws back in.

The bicycle was complete! It cried out for its gear. So I unzipped the body bag and removed the four panniers, handlebar bag, tent, sleeping bag and sleeping pad and loaded up the mule. I just had to test it out. Good thing I did. I didn't get two feet when the handlebar twisted hard under pressure and I nearly fell over. My unskilled hand had neglected to tighten the stem firmly. I was demoted instantly to my sure place in tool time history — idiot.

I tightened the gizmo (everything is a gizmo or whatchamacallit to the mechanically unwise) and mustered the courage to try again. I gave the handlebar a few hard tugs. It did not relent. I got on my bike and pedaled around the parking lot. The bike was happy. It was whole again. It was ready to ride. I deposited the bike box and padding in the dumpster.

Now I had to figure out where to go.

That wasn't too difficult. I had the address of the hostel in the city, but no idea how to get there. Inside the hotel was an English speaking desk clerk who knew the hostel's location. He produced a map for me and showed me how to get there. The map was in English. Obviously, Iceland is ready for visitors. The hostel was only five kilometers away, he said.

Kilometers would replace miles over the next three months. Kilos would replace pounds. Fahrenheit would be no more. Celsius was the way to go. Good-bye feet, inches and yards. Hello metric system and centimeters, meters and hectares.

The clerk circled the area where we were and drew a line from the hotel to the hostel. Easy enough to follow. The street names though, would be virtually unpronounceable to a dunce like me who was fresh off the plane.

Miklabraut, Kringlumyrarbraut and Sundlaugavegar were rattled off. My face went blank. I had no idea what he was saying when it came to the streets. I just smiled and nodded my head. I would do a lot of that in the next three months.

Instead of trying to tackle the new language, I immediately admitted defeat. I came to Iceland armed with three local words. One was *tak*. That means thank you. The other was the phrase *godin hundur*. That one means good dog. Every bicycle rider should know that one.

Pedaling the first few miles through Reykjavik was a blur of traffic and confusion. The confusion was mostly mine. But soon enough, I found the hostel, checked in and thought I'd sleep for awhile.

Wrong. Though I was familiar with hostels through travel during my teen-age years, I had forgotten that some of them close during the day. After a shower, I was out on the street again.

The first order of business was changing money. There's nothing like a stack of neat, crisp and green American currency. Do any travel outside of the country, even just to Canada, and see how drab American money really is. Our change becomes a nuisance. Elsewhere, change seems worth more. There are larger denominations. The paper money is more colorful and creative. Yet it still has the feel of play money and takes some time before you do currency conversions quickly in your head.

There is an immediate shock when you see prices. Instead of something costing say ten dollars, all of a sudden, it's six-hundred and seventy something. It doesn't matter what that something is, it's just that six-hundred and seventy is a hell of a lot more than ten, though they are really equal to each other. Good-bye dollar. Hello kronor. Good-bye gallon of gasoline. Hello liters of petrol. Not that I would need lots of it. I did need gasoline for my stove. Icelanders were paying around $3 a gallon for gas in the summer of 1996. Americans are ready to impeach the president when it goes above $1.25.

Another observation was obvious as I walked around the downtown area during the lunch hour and visited a few shops. Icelanders pay a bigger sales tax — a whopping 24 and a half percent.

Starting to feel the effects of no sleep, I made it back to the hostel before it opened. Still, there were other travelers. An Irishman who had

Early settlers in Iceland used available resources, like grass, to cover the roofs of their homes.

cycled the Ring Road four years ago was there. There was a New Zealand couple in Iceland for a month's vacation. Travelers can bond instantly. The questions began. The tales were spun, and I hadn't even been in Iceland for a day.

Even before the wheels started turning, the stories had started.

Once the wheels rolled at around 9:30 a.m. on May 21, they wouldn't stop rolling until they had touched four countries and the lives of people who still believe in dreams, hope, the human spirit and adventure.

The wheels were set in motion with no fanfare. The day began as it had ended the day before, with the media. Every other week I would call home to New Hampshire Public Radio and speak with morning host Jay O'Neal about the trip. That way, I could count on *real* English at least twice a month.

On this day, I met the sports editor of *Morganbladid* who came out to do a story. "I just wanted to come over and meet this crazy guy," he told me.

That crazy guy was me. I was crazy in that Icelanders still tend to view foreigners who attempt to cycle the Ring Road, or worse, cycle the roads in the interior once they are open, as a bit nuts. I didn't know why this was true at the time. I would find out later.

I sought out the interview because I wanted to see if I would get e-mail from Icelanders. I had read they were one of the top users of the

Iceland's roadside emergency shelters provide a place to wait out the ever-shifting weather.

Internet in the world. Not only would the adventure take place on the roads, but also in cyberspace. I'm not a big World Wide Web surfer. I don't want to spend too many hours in front of a screen. Please dismiss any visions you may have of me hooked up to the 'Net from a tent. I planned to use the computer to zap my columns to a newspaper, keep in touch with friends, record my diary and see if anyone anywhere was following along.

The interview completed, the journey began.

Reykjavik was soon left behind.

Scenery changed rapidly. The concrete buildings were gone. The shoulder of the road narrowed, and a dirt path would run parallel to the highway. Was it for walking? No. It was for horses. With riders in the distance, this was at first a strange sight. The horses have an unusual gait, the movements of which I had never seen before. Icelanders take much pride in their horses.

Heading east, I was 22 miles into the day before I came across one of the emergency huts scattered throughout the island to aid hikers, motorists and anyone caught in a jam during the ever-shifting weather.

This hut was called *Neydarskyli* and it was right by the road. The red and blue trimmed shelter was on a pontoon that made it mobile if need be. Its bright colors would stand out on the worst of days. It was strapped down to the ground with metal cables.

Inside were a number of useful items like a table, folding chairs, two bed-type couches, candles and even hooks to hang your clothing. A few candles were scattered about. There was a map on the wall with a yellow circle and X indicating the location. In the corner was a call box. Press a few buttons, and speak to the authorities to let them know you are there. Interestingly, there was also a food cache. On the menu was a dehydrated mutton, potato, onion and mushroom stew.

First aid items were thrown in too like bandages, safety pins, scissors, gauze and a safety blanket.

It's nice to know these places exist, but I hope to never have to use one. That is, unless I'm looking for complimentary accommodations on the fairest of nights.

Just as the weather is moody, so is the landscape. Two miles down from a mountain pass, the green returned and I gazed down upon a fertile valley and the small town of Hveragerdi. Neatness apparently counts in Iceland. Litter is virtually unseen and the streets of Hveragerdi were spotless. Neat little rows of homes stood proud. Also, if there wasn't a house, there was a greenhouse. Here, nearly half of the country's vegetables and flowers are grown in a place that relies heavily on imports (and it is reflected in the prices of items).

Iceland is known for its hot springs and geothermal activity. A restaurant advertised "Earth Cooking" and outside, a cauldron hung over the natural bubbling waters, steam spewing forth.

I would stop by the side of the road to touch its waters. To a New Englander, the steam looked like fog and I associated it with cold. But it was hot to the touch. What a smile it must have brought to the first settlers of Iceland who made a discovery which probably led to a permanent human population.

The road stretched into Selfoss where I met an Icelander who resembled a Nordic Ernest Hemingway. A white-bearded man with a baseball cap, he sat in his sport utility car, saw my bike by the market and started a conversation. He held out some grapes for me and told me last year he had cycled the Ring Road in 20 days. He was 70.

So, the stories began. At night, I sought the local campground for a place to sleep. The tourist season doesn't really start until the beginning of June. The campground was officially closed, but I could unofficially stay for free.

I wasn't the only one camping there. A German student also had his tent up. He was spending about three months walking around the country.

He had a large expedition-like tent with several stakes hammered into the ground. I asked him why he needed such a tent.

"You've never been to Iceland before," he said. "You'll see."

CHAPTER THREE

Beneath The Waterfall

The farmers waved from time to time. When truckers passed, it seemed they all had one hand on the wheel and the other hand on the cellular phone talking away in a language I didn't understand. Everything is dramatic in Iceland. With one revolution of the pedal you look at wooden posts that border farms and with the next you are staring miles ahead at a volcano named Helka and wonder what it would be like to be coated with ash and baked if the mound ever erupted. That's what Iceland is — a glacier on top of a volcano.

Farmlands, no doubt made that way with generations of sweat, muscle and prayer, gave way to black ash and cycling through a desert near the top of the world.

Then, a divine hand would draw a line on the island and on the other side there was green and yellow again.

Five waterfalls flowed ahead amidst the greenery. The map said this was Seljalandfoss. As I approached, the waterfalls grew. There was a road leading to them, and the largest one, over 120 feet high. Three picnic tables sat on the neat, green grass. It was still May, only the second day of cycling Iceland, and though the temperature couldn't have been more than 60, the sun was shining and the feeling was of paradise. The roar of the waterfall won over my attention, and I looked at it, watching the spray hit the air and mini-rainbows bouncing every which way.

This was a splendid place to be alone, but I wasn't.

Two figures cut behind the waterfall and were gone. I saw the narrow dirt path they were on and followed behind the falls. This was a place where legends were born. I could only imagine the birth of stories at a place like this.

Little did I know, I was minutes away from one of my own.

A sign back by the tables indicated there was a campground just down the road. In the distance, I could see tents.

Six or seven tents were on a green field at the base of a waterfall. The two figures had walked here. The tents were behind a house that had been built into the grass. When the first settlers arrived, that's how they made due with the environment. The homes were constructed into the land.

I hoped these guys spoke English.

I rode up and walked over to the 15 or so guys, big dudes in fatigues who were tossing around a football.

"Speak English?," I asked.

"That's all I speak," said one.

The next thing you know, I'm setting up camp beneath a cascading green waterfall with hidden passages that were once home to early Icelanders, and perhaps even the trolls and fairies of legend.

The campground was closed, but these guys were staying anyway. I felt safe.

That's because I was in good company. These were the Marines, stationed in Iceland.

These members of the United States Marine Security Forces Company were on three days of adventure training. It was a chance for them to get off the military base and explore the country, getting a dose of nature and culture.

They call it "the Rock." For one year, they must stay here, stationed just outside of Reykjavik at the air base at Keflavik.

They'll tell you about a winter wind so fierce it will lift up huge trash bins. They'll tell you about partying into the wee hours of the morning in Reykjavik.

And when they learn you are an American from New Hampshire, the doors of hospitality just open wide.

They came from all over the United States — Nevada, Massachusetts and Georgia. They had names like Blue, Doc and even Manwich. Manwich it turns out wasn't his real name. But when you've only been at your new base for three weeks, there is an initiation process one must go through. Thus, Manwich was born.

Marines have their own lingo. It seemed just as foreign to me as Icelandic as they "hit the rack." Of course, Marines are a breed apart and we would just stand around and talk, sentences punctuated by slang for forni-

The U.S. Marines stationed in Iceland camped by a waterfall, and later went sledding on the grass with the author. They also stocked him up with supplies.

cation and defecation and the silence cut by the sounds of flatulence. Smoking seemed to be popular.

When one noticed that an Icelandic family exploring the area had a soccer ball, he went over and asked to borrow it. Soon, four jackets on each side of a field under the waterfall became the boundary of a 60 yard soccer field.

Marty the civilian was asked to play.

Who knows what the score was. Who remembers how long we played. Not being much of a soccer player, I just stuck to the right side of the field and tried hard to stay away from the ball. Every once in a while a teammate actually passed it to me and I quickly kicked it away from me.

Some had tattoos. They played in heavy military boots. Their dog tags would dangle from their necks.

As a bunch, they were aggressive. One, who I'll call "Animal" was a monster in the goal. He would do flips after he would stop a goal. He would take the ball in the gut. He would slide and tackle the opposing team members in flagrant violation of any rule of soccer.

But hey, it was fun.

After the game, a few of the Marines were going to head over to the steep, grassy slopes for a little sledding. Armed with little more than a bedroll, they asked me to join in. We hiked up what had to be a 55 percent pitch to the top of the slopes. There, and I did this only once, we careened down with makeshift sleds on the bumpy grass to hoots and hollers. The others had to do it more than once. One had to do it backwards, without a mat, his hands clasped behind his head.

Perhaps a new sport was born that day — grass lugeing.

The Marines attacked this activity with zest and gusto. I was pretty tired, having already cycled 47 miles and then spending time running away from a soccer ball.

These guys didn't think twice about scampering up the slope and zipping down on a bedroll. Someone says go, and they go. All I can say is that I'm glad these guys are on our side.

Between the sledding and soccer, I seemed to have been accepted. Then again, a little foreign public relations goes a long way.

Before I left the next day, the Marines loaded me up with kindness in the form of food. I took two meal packets that were filled with oatmeal, fruit bars, nut raisin mix, cocoa, apple cider, chicken noodle soup, crackers, spoons, picnic meat, beef stew, brownie, granola bar and tea. Each packet had about 5,000 calories. These are what the Marines used in the field. Also in the packs were toilet paper and little pieces of gum. I was warned that the gum was also a mild laxative as all those calories tend to weigh a soldier down.

Doc, their medic, also gave me a bon voyage present. Into a plastic bag he threw two ace bandages, about a dozen gauze pads, a combination dressing, germicidal hand wipe, and about 40 tablets of pain relief medicine.

I immediately popped down the pain killers.

They were just kicking in as I rode away from the place where yet another story was born.

The magic from the Icelandic waterfalls caught up to me again on the day I left the Marines. It was a day with morning sun and glaciers in the landscape. The silence would be cut by the caws of the gulls which hovered and nested in the many cliffs above. Farms by the sea were common. Large boulders held forth in the middle of many flat areas. They apparently had rolled down from the cliffs above over the years but it was better to imagine them as being hurled by the gods of lore in some ancient game. Maybe they had come to rest in an early bowling contest or contest of skill. Perhaps two gods had competed over the attention of the stunning Icelandic women. The towering gods would lift the boulders. Look-

25

ing like Olympic athletes, they would grunt and hurl the boulder like a shot put. Maybe they whirled the rocks like a discus thrower. The winner won affection, while the loser was banished to the desolate interior — vast, cold and foreboding.

Once again, I saw a waterfall in the distance. This one was called Skogar and it stood over 100 feet high, making it one of the most impressive in the country. Legend has it that Prasi, the Viking who settled in Skogar, hid a chest of gold behind it. The chest disappeared. Only the chest's ring was found.

The waterfall was a good spot for lunch. Solitude left as a bus pulled up. From the bus came a wave of giggles, shouts and screams. The waterfall was a stop on a field trip for an elementary school. Though the teachers had planned to teach a bit about the waterfall, the lesson included a bit of an unscheduled English and geography course as well.

I was the subject of curiosity.

Let's face it. One look at me and you know I'm not of Scandinavian descent. The only stitch of blonde hair I have is in my mind. There aren't too many locals at the top of the world with scrubby red beards and receding brown hairlines. I'm not exactly rugged and angular either.

I look the part of the foreigner in Iceland.

So, though I was minding my own business, soon, the bravest of the school kids started eyeing me and making their way over to me. Their shouts were just white noise. Eye contact was made. I smiled.

The bravest one, a boy of maybe 11, jabbered something my way.

I smiled.

He was with two other boys. They looked perplexed. They gabbed among themselves.

The brave one spoke again.

"How are you?," he asked in English.

"Just fine. How about you," I answered.

He said he was fine too.

This brief exchange seemed to elevate the brave one in his little crowd. That he was able to communicate in a strange tongue to a stranger with a bicycle was a colossal accomplishment. No doubt this boy would one day be king.

The exchange made the entourage more animated and they seemed to tell the brave one things to ask me.

"Where are you from?," asked the brave one.

I answered "America."

This the group understood. More children dared to come closer. Some of the teachers took notice. The impromptu, outdoor class by the waterfall was growing.

Students from an elementary school crowd around the author's bicycle after an impromptu outside classroom experience.

"How far do you go?," inquired the brave one.

I answered in miles.

This meant someone had to convert to kilometers. Guess there was some math lessons in there too.

I soon learned that this was the second to last day of school for the students, and that the brave one had once been to Miami, Florida. A few of his compatriots then thought it was safe to also ask questions.

They asked me what I thought of Iceland. They asked me what I carried in the bags. They asked me about my favorite sports teams.

Then one caught me off guard.

"Do you know Bart Simpson?," one asked.

I stared at the child with a bit of disbelief. I wasn't terribly friendly with many cartoon characters.

"No, I don't."

"What about Homer?," was the follow-up.

"Nope, not him either."

America exports many desirable items to others in the world. Blue jeans seem to be hot items. High-tech basketball and running shoes are sought after. Sure, America beams its television shows all over the globe for the masses to see. But are "The Simpson's," a family led by a lovable buffoon and his wiseass kid, something we want the world to see? Are Homer and Bart synonymous with America? I hope not.

***Open air racks of fish hang to dry. Icelanders say once dried, they are best
eaten with butter.***

So, I decided to turn the tables a bit and ask them about their culture,
in particular a food item I had purchased at the grocery store in Hella.

I took out the *hardfiskur*, or hardfish, from my saddlebag. The fish is
dried haddock, cod or catfish and is ready to eat, straight from the package. The fish isn't exactly cooked. It is dried. The fish is caught, gutted
and hung out to dry on racks for a few months. That makes it a bit like a
fish jerky. It resembles parchment and is an Icelandic delicacy, right up
there with *svid*, which is singed sheep heads. I was carrying hardfish,
though not any *svid*. Apparently, May isn't *svid* season.

There were now over a dozen children staring at me, listening to the
question and answer session. A few giggles surfaced as I took out the fish.

"Do you like this?," I asked the children.

They all seemed to nod their heads.

"Do you?," one asked.

I told them I thought it tasted a little strange, like dried paper. And
that I found it very difficult to bite through the skin.

There was silence, then laughter started to make its way through the
children.

"You don't eat the skin," said the brave one. "Only weird people eat
the skin. You are to eat it with butter."

Well, that I, the uninformed foreigner, ate hardfish with skin on and
without butter, was a bit too much. The laughter seemed to overtake the

din of the waterfall. I could just see them going home to their parents who would ask how school was today.

"Oh, we met an American on a bicycle who was carrying a computer, mama."

"That's nice."

"He ate hardfish with the skin on."

"I told you to stay away from strangers."

It was time for the children to go, but not before the teachers wanted to get a picture of the students with this gastronomic oddity. The 25 or so children surrounded me and my bike. The teachers took a few shots.

As the children got on the bus, some said good-bye to me in English. Others said, *bless*.

Bless means good-bye in Icelandic. I certainly felt blessed as the bus pulled away and the waterfall's magic worked its wonders again.

CHAPTER FOUR

Honorary Viking For A Day

"Sam. Hello, Sam. Sam, are you in there?," a voice called.

Sam, who is Sam, I thought. And why is that voice looking for him.

"Sam, hello. Sam," the voice continued.

From inside the tent, my thoughts turned to Sam and wished he would answer. Sam was interrupting my mid-day snooze in Iceland's largest national park, Skaftafell. My journey had taken me 220 miles thus far, and I was having a rest day.

Actually, it hadn't been much of a rest day at all. The Icelandic rains had fallen, and fallen hard for a day or so. Just the night before, I spent the night in a hotel in Kirkjubæjarklaustur and used it more as a drying room than as a room of luxury. The night before, it had been a campground in the coastal village of Vik and dinner had been grilled sausages under high cliffs with birds flying above, taking turns playing aerial darts and using my tent as the target.

My gear was finally drying out. I had learned a great trick for drying out my wet hiking boots overnight. Stuff them with either newspaper or toilet paper and in the morning, they are dry and toasty.

The fact that Skaftafell National Park was closed hadn't dampened my spirits to stay there. I was not alone. Icelanders and tourists were camping for free in late May. The bathrooms were open. The water was running. The hot air dryers were operational. The grocery store was being stocked with canned food. Life was good.

That morning, I had done some exploring, by foot, in the park and came across a few interesting tales and people.

Tragedy and humor sometimes combine forces for the name of a natural site. Take the Hundafoss, I stumbled upon. The country's largest national park was once a manor farm during the Middle Ages. Travelers going to the farm would cross the river near the edge of the waterfall. When the water was high, dogs were known to be washed over the edge. Thus the name — "Dog's Fall."

Now, some 60,000 visitors annually make the journey to the park in Southeast Iceland to view the Hundafoss and another unusual fall, the Svartifoss, plus gaze upon the biggest glacier in all of Europe, Vatnajökull.

"Skaftafell National Park is an area which can accommodate almost anybody. You can take a trip to Svartifoss that is about one hour which is uphill but fairly easy. Then, we also have the climbers who want to go on the glacier. The biggest part of the park is actually covered by the glacier," said park warden Stefan Benediktsson. He was one of the early visitors too.

The park, and many parts of this country, is like Mother Nature's smorgasbord, a masterpiece of seemingly impossible contrasts of nature. Towering mountains, imposing glaciers, the chirping of birds and lush vegetation are all at home in the park. The Skaftafell landscape was created by glacial action and water erosion. The Icelandic government declared about 340 square miles of the area as a national park on September 15, 1967, and later more than tripled its size on July 27, 1984.

Amazingly, there is no admission to the park which is open from June 1 to September 15. Camp sites are reasonable. Park staff conduct hikes during the summer. According to Benediktsson, there are no nature programs at the park in English, but members of the staff are bilingual and do answer questions.

A walk on the marked paths along the gulches for a look at the waterfalls is a must for every park visitor. The most majestic is Svartifoss, or the "Black Falls." The waters plunge over a wall of symmetrical columnar basalt that looks like giant church organ pipes.

The strange black and brown columns were formed during gradual cooling of a layer of molten lava. The water has since broken its way through the lava crust and created the falls.

Iceland's weather can change quicker than the snap of a finger. Benediktsson says the best time to visit Skaftafell is in July when there are fairly warm days and nights in the 60 degree range.

Also, visitors still get a taste of a northern delight — the midnight sun. In July, visitors to the Far North can still enjoy 24 hours of daylight and the vegetation is at its peak.

Walkers in the park will notice several types of birds like the red-breasted thrush, buntings and wren. One peculiar type of bird makes a sound reminiscent of what a spaceship might make.

"That's the snipe," said Benediktsson. "This sounds like an alien. When she is flying over the area and diving, she spreads out her tail and the sound is the vibration of the air going through the feathers of the tail."

Skaftafell is also the gateway to the behemoth glacier that covers 11 percent of Iceland — Vatnajökull. The glacier itself is about 65,000 square miles, nearly one-third the size of Holland. The park sits on a tongue of the glacier called Öræfajökull; perched on it is Iceland's largest mountain, Hvannadalsnukur. At 6,950 feet, it is slightly higher than the highest peak in the northeastern United States — New Hampshire's Mount Washington.

Visitors can walk up to the glacier or peer into it from a point called Sjonarnipa. The hike there from the campsite is roughly four miles roundtrip. It's possible to combine this hike with walks to the falls as well.

On a misty day, the gray clouds came down to cover much of the glacier. But small windows opened on occasion for a look at the blackened masses topped with spring snow. The path is clearly marked with colorful stakes and the effort was worth it. From Sjonarnipa visitors can look out upon a part of Vatnajökull with its black and white checkerboard markings. There are layers of blue and deep, deep crevasses where if you were walking on the snow, one slip can mean tragedy.

I did not become a statistic that day. For that, I was thankful as I danced in and out of sleep in my tent.

Then the "Sam" calling began.

After a few shouts, I zipped myself out from the tent to peek outside and wondered if Sam was in a tent next to me or something.

Two tall Icelanders met my gaze as I stuck my head out into the grayness.

"Sam, we thought you were in there," said one.

"My name isn't Sam," I said.

The two looked at each other and engaged in conversation in their native tongue so I had no idea what was going on. After a few exchanges, it was explained to me that one of them had recognized me from a newspaper article in the paper *Morganbladid*, thought my name was Sam, and wanted to invite me on a "walk."

The pair — Eiki and Markus — were climbers. They, along with their five friends, were members of a search and rescue team located outside of Reykjavik, in the town of Hafnarfjördur. The seven were doing some hiking and climbing in the Skaftafell area. In the early evening, they were planning to go for a "walk" to look for an ice cave a farmer had

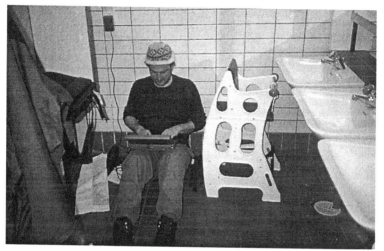

Where there is power, there is an office. The author finds a unique use for the men's room at Skaftafell National Park.

told them about.

I accepted. You never turn down an invitation from a local to show you around, even if you are damn tired on a rest day.

I caught a few hours of sleep, before the "walk" which turned out to be some sort of ritual for admission into the Viking Initiation Club, if there is such a thing.

The throbbing bass line from The Knack's "My Sharona" blared from the monster red van as it shot down Highway One in search of the ice cave. In the tape deck was the soundtrack from the off-color, but critically acclaimed "Pulp Fiction." When language is a barrier, music becomes the international communicator.

Eight of us were in the van. These were Markus and Eiki's friends — fellow rescuers and climbers. The seven ranged in age from 19 to 22 and were at various stages in life from student to factory worker. Aside from Markus and Eiki, there was Joi, Agusta, Anita, Gardar and Helgi. In addition to the climbers, there was a whole floor filled with gear. They had ice axes, crampons, rope, harnesses, backpacks, plastic insulated mountain-

33

eering boots, helmets, carabiners and first aid equipment. I had on everything I brought with me which didn't include anything remotely resembling crampons, ice axes and harnesses.

I had my camera though.

Above the din, we peppered each other with questions as "Jungle Boogie" roared from the speakers. Since they were climbers, they knew about the area I came from and wanted to know about climbing the highest peak in the northeast, Mt. Washington, and a bit about the rock ledges like White Horse and Cathedral in the area. Joi, one of the more animated of the group, had a penchant for chewing snuff and would chew, then spit into a cup, and chuck it out the window. Being hospitable, he offered me some.

Not wanting to offend, I joined in.

Gardar guided the vehicle off the road after we had gone through maybe half the tape and onto what Icelanders might call dirt roads and all others might call wilderness. Four-wheel drive is mandatory for negotiating these so-called roads. Up steep pitches, over water and down steeper inclines, Gardar drove over what I saw as nothing; he saw a road.

Now the van was rocking and rolling and it wasn't because of the music.

Soon enough, the van comes to a spot where the climbers believe we can start looking for the ice cave.

We leave the van and a few of them start peering through binoculars to look for the cave.

The others walk over to a glacial river. I look at the direction the binoculars are pointing. I see the gushing, frigid river. I see a metal basket on one side of the river. I see a cable, over 150 feet long, reaching over this rushing river.

You don't need a translator to figure out what was going on.

They start taking out the equipment from the van.

The thought of being a monkey on a swing was not amusing to me.

The basket would be launched and the basket rider would pull himself over the waters to the other side. But closer inspection of the metal basket revealed a most incredible finding. The cage was padlocked and couldn't be moved. We couldn't use the basket.

Too bad, I thought with a great sense of relief.

However, these Icelanders are a hearty breed. They are resourceful. And they had climbing equipment.

All it took were harnesses, carabiners and rope. In about 15 minutes, the first of them was hanging upside down, several feet above the raging waters, pulling himself along the cable in a mountaineering move called a Tyrolian traverse. Markus was on belay. Joi pulled himself across.

Members of an Icelandic search and rescue team cross the largest glacier in Europe.

Then Helgi.

"Soon it will be your turn," said Eiki.

I looked at Gardar. I looked at Anita. I looked at Agusta.

I looked at my imaginary watch.

"Oh, look at the time," I said. "Won't it be getting dark soon?"

That's one excuse you can't use in the "Land of the Midnight Sun" during the spring and summer months.

"I don't have a harness," I said.

The four were just having fun with me. I noticed Helgi and Joi were returning.

"The ice cave isn't here," said Anita. "It is another place."

Gardar had been on the cellular phone with the farmer who told them about the cave. We headed back into the van and rocked and rolled some more.

We arrived near the spot of the ice cave. We would just have to climb on a glacier to get there. A glacier with crevasses. A glacier with holes where one slip meant see ya'.

We split up.

I went with Anita, Agusta and Markus.

Markus handed me an ice axe and imparted four words of wisdom to me: "First think, then do."

"You think. You do. I follow," I said.

This was not like hiking some of the easier well-marked trails of the White Mountain National Forest back home. There were no trails here. There were no signs. This was a place where skill and experience absolutely, positively mattered. I had done early spring hiking in Tuckerman Ravine, a glacial cirque on the eastern side of Mount Washington that holds snow into summer. I had traveled up there with packs to do some skiing. But there was a difference. I had been prepared and had the proper equipment.

Now I had bike clothing on. Climbing equipment was not part of my arsenal.

But I had to trust who I was with. Reasoning told me they would not take me out on a place where I did not belong.

Up through time we traveled. A glacier is nothing but time frozen. First the path was through dirt-covered snow. As we continued, with Markus leading the way with two ski poles, plodding and checking each step, the surface became cleaner and more majestic. The black glacier turned to white and was a massive checkerboard desert. The horizon seemed endless as we crunched on jewels. The sun cast an eerie glow which added to the magic of the hike.

In the distance, I saw Eiki who, along with Gardar, Helgi and Joi, had taken another route to the ice cave.

They had found the cave and had already been inside. They also had the time to shovel a few quick steps for an easy descent. We stepped down into the glacier and a new blue world. A dazzling, spectacular cave awaited. This was like an underground diamond mine. A small rivulet wound its way through. Our voices echoed. Breathing brought a mist. Eiki placed an ice axe on the ground and took pictures of it to prove the group had been there.

Soon we were leaving the cave that would melt over the next few weeks. All of us started to head back to the van.

The trip to the cave, with added detour of the first stop, had taken longer than anticipated. Tiredness started to permeate the group and it was decided to take an alternate route back.

This involved crossing four glacial streams. We all know that water freezes at 32 degrees Fahrenheit. Yet that day, in a strange phenomenon which only happened to me, and only during those four river crossings, the freezing temperature of water dropped. It took a nose dive, plummeted, dropped like a lead balloon to zero. No, below zero. Even below, below zero.

Cold can be defined as walking barefooted through a gushing river that is flowing from a glacier. Stupidity can also be defined as walking barefooted through a gushing river that is flowing from a glacier.

Holding onto ropes the leaders would toss across, we conquered the waters. Since the seven had changes of clothing, they thought nothing of walking right through. I had but one pair of boots. So I thought I would keep them dry.

After the first crossing over smooth rock which seemed to take forever, I also realized I had but two feet. It would be nice to have them with me for the rest of the trip.

So the next three crossings were quicker with the boots on. Still, the cold drained what little strength I had left.

A thermos of hot cappuccino was back in the van. Joi gave me more snuff.

Soaked, I didn't say much on the ride back.

Near midnight, the seven set up a feast back at the campground. I tried some Icelandic food like *flatkokur* and *hangikjot* which is flat bread and smoked meat.

With my energy drained and gravity winning the war with my eyelids, I said good night to the search and rescue team and went to my tent with Anita's words ringing in my head.

"So now you are Viking," she said with a laugh in the van.

Yes, but a wet one.

CHAPTER FIVE

Lighthouse Soup
And The Mayor

The omen should have been the cap blowing off my head as soon as I stepped outside the Hotel Blafell in Breiodalsvik.

I had been forced into the hotel the day before because of the wind. The wind had been dancing around me for a few days now. It was a wind that laughed, that had a persistent jab, that forced me to the ropes, gave me an instant of hope and then crushed me. The wind was deafening, angry and unmerciful. This was an in-your-face, take no prisoners wind. Then to compound the situation, sheets of rain, thick king-sized sheets, started to fall from the darkened sky.

There was more.

Mechanical problems came for a visit. My chain snapped. A spoke had broken and a clamp holding my front rack cracked from the harsh Icelandic road. Quick fixes like riding one link short, using duct tape for the clamp and affixing a spare string spoke were in order.

Difficulties arise on the road. You just put your head down and ride. Or, you get off your bike and walk.

Or, you make soup.

The unseen but ever-present wind was too much of a force. It proved too much to pedal in, and up ahead was a lighthouse. Near the lighthouse was a utility shack. Both the lighthouse and utility shack were closed. I opted to stay out of the wind by staying on one side of the brown shack. I was also hungry and assembled one of those one-pot wonder meals that are only good while traveling. Out came the stove and in went the water, beef bouillon, a can of tuna fish and multi-colored bowtie macaroni. Soon, a new delicacy was born, Lighthouse Soup.

In between sips of the hot soup, I would glance around the bend of the shack and be rewarded with a knock-out punch from the wind. Rest was good.

Inadvertently, I had left the front portion of my bicycle exposed to the wind. I put my bicycle helmet on the saddlebags and it was now in the wind's unforgiving path.

I was startled to see the wind lift up my bicycle helmet and toss it without any effort into the rocks by the shack. As I went to retrieve it, the sack which I carried my stove in took off. There I was, trying to decide which one to go after, looking like a squirrel trying to cross the road with the onset of a car coming. Looking this way, then that, going this way, then that. I settled on the helmet first as it was starting to go quite a ways down an embankment.

I scurried about and retrieved both items. Back by the shack, I looked at the helmet. I was shocked. The impact of the helmet smashing against the rock had cracked it! A part of the styrofoam behind the right ear had nearly been torn off. Glad I wasn't in that helmet at the time.

This wind wasn't giving up. With both the lighthouse and shack closed, I had to wait this out. The wind was too powerful to fight on a bicycle.

So I wrestled with it by putting up the tent.

There was no room for mistakes in setting up the self-supporting tent. One slip and part of it could take off like a kite without a string and head straight into the Atlantic Ocean. The first thing to do was pick up a few rocks to use as weights.

The ground cloth went down with some effort, the wind wrapping it around my body, hugging my face in what could be its attempt at suffocation. One rock went down on the cloth. Then another. Soon, all four corners were fastened.

Now came the tent. First, the two poles were snapped together. The thought was to anchor down the tent with stakes. Unfortunately, the ground was hard. The first stake, pounded down with a rock, bent. The second stake, pounded down with a rock, bent. The plan changed. Quickly, the poles were inserted into the tent. It was like blowing up a balloon and now there was more mass for the wind to toy with. The wind tried to launch the tent to the moon. I hung on for life. It smacked me around like a punching bag. I would pull it down and try to use the rocks as makeshift anchors. This American comedy continued for what seemed several minutes, until the wind relented, probably tired from laughing so hard, and I scampered in with pad and sleeping bag for some rest.

Wrong.

The wind picked up and continued its rock 'em, sock 'em tactics. Jab. Jab. Upper cut. Hook. The pounding was persistent. The tent walls flapped relentlessly. The wind efficiently tossed aside the rocks as makeshift stakes. The wind easily lifted the lightest areas of the tent up into the air. I was holding on for the windiest ride of my life.

It was clear no rest would be had in the tent. So almost as comically, all the parts were disassembled and into the wind I headed.

Sections of the Icelandic landscape can tantalize bicyclists. The fjords can go deep into the folds of the land. A town up ahead, across the water, can appear to be only five miles away. But in reality, it can be 10, 20 or 30 miles, in, around, up, down and over. It's like cycling across your hand. Instead of going directly from the thumb to the pinkie, you ride along the outline of the hand, pedaling the roller coaster to index finger, middle ringer, ring finger and finally pinkie.

Breiodalsvik was easily seen. The little fishing village, in a cove of the same name, had all the necessities for me — hotel, store, camping. How I had hoped one of its inhabitants had seen me and offered to put me in a boat for a ride across the bay.

It didn't happen.

Exhausted, into the hotel I headed. Out of the wind's howl. Out of its' wrath, might and fury. I relished the silence that night and only hoped the morning would be less punishing.

But it wasn't.

The plan was a 54 mile ride to the town of Egilsstadir. At Breiodalsvik, the Ring Road leaves the coast and heads inland. Ocean breezes account for much of the wind. The thinking was perhaps the wind would cut me a break as I pedaled away from the coast.

Wrong.

My wool cap flew off as I stepped out from the hotel.

The decision was made to press on.

In only a few miles, the wind nearly brought me to tears. It never took a break, shouting at me the whole day. Yelling, screaming, not letting me ride. Experience took the day off. Stupid as I was, I just walked. This should have been a day to lay low. To wait. To be patient. Though I had interviewed climbers of the world's highest peaks, I had not yet learned from them. Their stories had a similar thread. When the weather is bad, you wait. There are times to wait. There are times to move on.

The summit isn't the only adventure. The spirit of adventure lives in the climb, the journey. I should have let this hellish wind settle down. Read, meet the people, then pedal.

No. I didn't. The breaks in the monotony came when I rested, when I tried to set up my tent but couldn't get out of the wind. I ended up wrapping myself in my tent fly to get a little rest.

The other break in the monotony came when a dog followed me. It was white and cream colored and reminded me of my childhood mutt named Brandy. The dog just wouldn't go home. Of course, the dog was a sheep dog and showed me it could move its flock. It weaseled under the barbed wire fences and followed me as I walked. At times the dog seemed more interested in trying to catch, or at least chase, the Canadian geese in this huge canyon and meadow I was taking my bike for a walk in. Then the dog would be back. How far it followed, I don't know. But it didn't return fast enough for its owners.

I tried telling the dog to go home, but of course, it didn't understand me. Dogs here don't speak English. They speak Icelandic and the only words I knew were good dog. Perhaps that's why the dog followed for so long.

The owners came by in a pick-up, said a word or two in Icelandic and the dog left me to get in the truck. It was gone.

I continued cursing my stupidity. Why I didn't knock on one of the farm doors and ask for shelter I don't know. I had the opportunity.

The sky was darkening and perhaps it was my lack of energy, my howling at the wind too, but I felt colder. Night was falling, the wind still prevailed.

There was still beauty around me, but tears were near. There was one more farm left in this canyon before the gravel road took a sharp hike up a mountain pass. I would knock on the door at that farm and babble like a stupid foreigner and beg for mercy to be saved from this evil force.

Maybe a dozen cars had passed me this day. It had been nearly two hours since a vehicle had passed. If ever there was a day for a ride, this was it.

A new, sparkling pick-up truck stopped a few yards before the last farm house.

I went around to the driver's side window.

"Hello," I said to the man who rolled down the window.

"Where are you going?," the man asked in English.

"Just up the Ring Road," I answered

"To Egilsstadir?," he asked.

"Hopefully," I said.

"Would you like a lift?," he asked.

Those five words restored my energy. The bike was stuffed into the back of the truck and entering the cab was like a sanctuary. For the first time in 11 hours, the wind fell silent.

"Thank you," I said. "You just saved me from my own stupidity."

He just smiled and took off.

"Seatbelt please," were the words spoken.

The chitchat began. The man, dressed in green — green shirt, green pants, green vest — had just been in Reykjavik, where on the way back, the weather had turned foul and he had to wait seven hours for a sandstorm to pass before the road was re-opened.

The road climbed through a snow-covered pass. The man said he hoped the road was open. The sun's night glow made the mountains even more like a scene on a huge movie screen. We talked about America, and how he had just been to Philadelphia. He had been to Baltimore, New York, Washington and Boston too.

"Are you retired," I asked.

"Me. No. I am a farmer, just a little bit. It's a hobby," he said.

"Then, what do you do?"

"I'm a mayor," he said.

So that is how I met Magnus Thorsteinsson, mayor of the 200 person village of Morgarfjördur Eystra. He has been mayor for quite some time. First elected in 1974, he hadn't lost since then, he said. Every four years there is an election. He doesn't have much competition sometimes.

"Sometimes nobody runs," he said. "I used to be a real farmer, but when I was elected mayor, I didn't have time any more."

One of the mayor's duties had brought him to Reykjavik that day. He was there to take delivery of the town's new vehicle, the pick-up truck we were riding in. It had just been delivered to Iceland. Not only was it used to haul around town employees and their tools, but to transport the town's children to school.

And that's how a bicycling foreigner became the first passenger in the town's new school bus. Though not in school anymore, he was still a pupil, being taught by forces of nature much more powerful than he.

CHAPTER SIX

Touching The Circle

More birds than people live on the Arctic island of Grimsey, but that doesn't bother Sigrun Oladottir. Oladottir, who runs the Basar guest house on the west end of this three mile long, 1.5 mile wide rock, was born and raised in this community of about 120 people.

"We are not isolated at all," she said, putting the finishing touches on cleaning the hotel sign. "Here, we have very good communication. The ferry comes two times a week year-round. A plane comes every day in the summer and three times a week in winter. It is very easy to get on and off."

To reach Grimsey, one must first reach Akureyri. The coastal town is a welcome retreat from the sheep, horses and cows of rural Iceland. The north is just beginning to wake up from winter. The fields are mostly brown, though green does make an appearance. Towering mountains protect the town of 14,000 as clouds of gray hide the summits, squaring off the hills like bunt cakes with snowy ravines looking like fingers of frosting.

The town is known as the "capital" of northern Iceland. It boasts a ski area on its outskirts and a fine walking area downtown with restaurants, shops and galleries.

At 10 a.m. sharp, a bus left the Akureyri terminal with two British tourists and one American onboard bound for the Arctic island. Another passenger was later picked up. The weather, good for Iceland in June, was partly cloudy with spots of sun.

Outside of Akureyri, the fishing port of Dalvik was alive with children. Just out from school which ends in May, they were clad in winter jackets and hats, playing soccer. The smell of the fish plant smacks travelers getting off the bus after a half hour ride. The dock workers were loading the yellow and blue trimmed boat with bounty destined for Grimsey and the Arctic Circle. Four cars were lifted onto the boat by a crane, the vehicles twirling in the air as workers yelled instructions to each other, making the autos look more like kites and toys than a ton of metal. Mail, packages and one, lone 21 speed dirtied green mountain bike also made the journey.

Grimsey is the northernmost point in Iceland, located just above the Arctic Circle at 66 degrees, 33 minutes north. The circle actually runs right through the middle of the island. There's a sign that marks it, just outside of Oladottir's front door which is also by the airport. The signpost points to places like New York, Tokyo and Moscow, all so far away. To reach the island with just over 100 inhabitants, humans that is, the boat navigated the chilly Atlantic waters of the Eyjafjördur. The sun shining, the squared off mountains lining the fjord on both sides, the blue Icelandic flag with its red cross waved in the wind as the 11 passengers in the comfortable cabin bided their time, communicating in a smattering of languages.

Bird, hundreds, flock around the islands. An orange neon lighthouse is passed. Hold on tightly as you head outside the cabin and up the steep steps to the deck. Everything is vibrant. The salt air is invigorating.

Grimsey is several miles off the Icelandic coast. At the docks, fishermen weigh in their catch at the end of the day, hooks attached to a crane lift the giant containers filled with over 600 pounds of fresh fish. The lighthouse is at the east end. There is the church, but the priest doesn't live on the island. He's in Akureyri and must commute. There's a school too. Children can go to school there until they are 12. Then they go to boarding school in Dalvik.

There's a store which also houses the gasoline pumps, the post office, the swimming pool and maybe twenty or so homes. Most of island's residents are in the fishing industry. When I was there, Oladottir's little daughter was off to a birthday party.

Only the southern part of the island is settled with people. The rest is uninhabited. At least, people don't live there. There are cliffs, and there are birds. The birds live there to nest, to wait, to eat and to fly.

The birds are why visitors flock to Grimsey. It's a bird watcher's delight to see the gulls, the razor bills, fumars, kittiwakes and the aggressive Arctic terns.

But the bird in the spotlight is the puffin. Perhaps one of nature's most formal looking flying creatures, the puffins look something like Toucan Sam on a morning cereal box. Orange beaked and orange footed, the puffin has a white breast and what looks like a black tuxedo making them ready for a night on the town.

What's unique about Grimsey, is that you can get very close to the birds before they take off after seeing your shadow.

The birds aren't too difficult to find. Just follow the red plastic balls outside Oladottir's house and go through the field. But watch out for the terns. Although Alfred Hitchcock's thriller "The Birds" was not filmed here, new heads attract the terns and they are nasty. They'll dive and bomb humans. One came down and tweaked the cap on my head. Even putting up my hood didn't stop them.

And if you are on a bicycle, the flying menaces will do everything they can to mark their spot on you.

After braving the mean terns, visitors can see scores of other birds soaring, nesting and feeding by the high cliffs.

"Ninety percent of the people who come to Grimsey are bird watchers. That's the first factor. The other people come for the midnight sun. I'm always booked on June 21. That's the longest day of the year. They watch the midnight sun. They come for the beauty of the lifestyle and for the peace and quiet," Oladottir said.

So if June 21 is rapidly approaching, better make that reservation. The 12 bedrooms are booked up fast.

CHAPTER SEVEN

The Stripes Of Home

There was something strange about the flags waving in the wind. Nine flags flew in Blönduos. Up against the blue sky, the colors representing the countries of Iceland, Austria, Belgium, the United Kingdom, France, Holland, Ireland, Italy and Germany all rippled in the wind.

At least one was missing.

The flags were waving in the breeze outside the office of the campground in this small town of around 1200 in northwest Iceland at the mouth of the glacial river called Blanda. Merchant ships used to dock here and in 1876, it was designated as an official trading center in the country. So, there is a bit of international panache in its history.

The campground was at the end of another one of those heaven and hell days of Icelandic biking. Overcast skies welcomed the morning and the hills were long out of Varmahlid, a small town which seemed to grow out of a crossroads.

Yet long downhills were the reward and wind remained at my back. The wind wasn't friendly for long though. The road switches direction in what seems like an instant and the wind follows suit. Bang, the wind turns from buddy to enemy.

The low-lying clouds eventually burned away and the sun shared the sky with blue. Blönduos, was at first hard to spot, but appeared after a turn in the hill. Then there were the flags.

At the campground I met Ofeigur Gestsson. He runs the place.

We took a look at the flags.

"Why isn't there an American flag up there?," I asked.

"When people come or the day after, I put up their flag," he said.

"Why do you do that?," he was asked.

"I think it's interesting for them. When I am visiting other countries, I think it's interesting to see my flag. It is warm. It shows that we are thinking about them," he said.

Gestsson's flags have been gracing the skies of Blönduos for only a short time. What could become a tradition, started in the summer of 1995. Gestsson has 27 flags from 27 different nations. You might think those flags would cover tourists from all over the world and you would almost be right. But there is one flag Gestsson doesn't have — Singapore.

I told Gestsson I would be staying at the campground that night. He informed me it was still early in the season and he wasn't charging people yet. Seems he still had some finishing touches to take care of on the grounds and buildings. That was fine with me so I went across the street to enjoy another Icelandic tradition — the swimming pool.

If every there has been a saving grace in this wild and beautiful place, it is the warm waters of the over 80 swimming pools for the country's inhabitants. For a measly $2.50 or $3 per visit, guests can swim in pools of all shapes and sizes. This one had a Jacuzzi outside, or as Gestsson said "a hot pot with pressure."

Into the hot pot with pressure I went and the day's road dust would fade away. Inside I met two women, one from Sweden and the other from Germany, who now live and work in Iceland. Sharing a Jacuzzi with someone speaking another language isn't so bad really. Since you can't understand what they are saying, their words just blend in with the jets for some background noise.

After awhile you ask if they speak English, and they did, and talk turned to the community and travel. Then you bring up that you are on a bicycle and they say, "Oh, you're one of those crazy ones."

It being Sunday the pool closes at 4 p.m. Soon the jets ceased firing and the pool attendant came out to announce it was time to lock up.

After taking another shower, I gathered my belongings and walked back across the street. The nine flags were ripping across the sky. There was nothing strange about them now. The flag from Belgium was no longer there. It had been replaced by the red, white and blue of home.

47

CHAPTER EIGHT

The Tent Man

If it hadn't been for a cold New Zealand biker, I never would have met the "tent man."

The man from Down Under was the twelfth cyclist I had spotted along the Ring Road. He, along with other early-season riders from the Netherlands, Switzerland, Canada and Germany, had been out and about on their own trips. The Canadians, from Prince Edward Island, had misjudged the country's terrain, and never even came close in their attempt to circle the island in two weeks. The Dutch riders were two delightful artists I met in Akureyri. They had opted to do a little cycling, and when the wind roared, hopped on a bus. The two, Anita and Marika, had seen me from their bus window and decided if we were ever to meet, they would buy me a cup of coffee.

The coffee, consumed in an Akureyri campground, was among the finest I've tasted.

But this nameless New Zealand biker, even on a warm (50ish) June day, was complaining about the cold. He had just spent time cycling in California and Nevada, so the sharp drop in temperature made him shiver.

We spend about a half hour by the road exchanging tales and observations. We spoke about Icelandic names, how only 10 percent of Icelanders have family names. They use a system of patronymics where the first name of the father is used with son or daughter. So Jonsson, means son of Jon and names like Halldorsdottir means daughter of Halldor.

We spoke about the inexpensive tubes of caviar for sale, and how being an English speaker heading into a grocery store makes your self-esteem take a nose dive because it takes twice as long to find things you can't locate because you can't read the aisle signs. Then when you think you've found the right aisle, you can't read the package.

He learned about what lay ahead for him — splendid isolation, areas with pock-marked snow, the geo-thermal activity of Myvatn, the bustling town of Akureyri, and sheer adventure. We both had discovered the joys of the country's pools and the fact that you could actually buy a half of loaf of bread! For the bicycling budget traveler, this discovery made squished bread moot.

I learned, that about two miles ahead, was a junction. At that junction was a sign for a ferry. Via the Ring Road, it would be another 60 miles or so back to Reykjavik, along a fjord. If I made a right at the junction, it would be about 10 miles into Akranes, among Iceland's largest fishing ports, and a ferry to Reykjavik. The ferry cost about $12. He raved about sampling the Icelandic coastline via the ferry. We parted ways and the adventures continued.

The sign was there all right. A little boat indicated there was indeed a ferry in Akranes. There was a spot to pull over, and it was there, I weighed the options at this decision junction. The day was early, and I was fresh. The wind was cooperating, and to press on would not be a problem. Indeed, the map showed a fjord. I had seen fjords. Beautiful as they are, they are also sometimes cruel and deceptive for the cyclist. Time was not a factor, as there was plenty of it to get to Reykjavik and a flight to Norway for the next leg of the Arctic trip.

Money certainly wasn't the issue. Nor was the issue of not completing a loop around Iceland. I hadn't. By accepting a ride in the pick-up truck turned school bus, that goal had been snuffed days before.

The ride to Reykjavik would probably be pleasant. The great motivator, though, was the wind. I wouldn't have to pedal against any of it if it decided to blow in my face. I would see the same fjord, except from a different angle.

Decision made, I pressed on into town. On the outskirts, horses galloped in the distance behind a backdrop of knife-edged mountains. Nothing but clean was seen in the streets of Akranes. Like in towns before, teen-agers were out at work, sweeping the streets, cutting lawns, bagging clippings. This is what they did during the summer. The government puts them to work, and pays them. If they were complaining, I couldn't understand them.

The tourist office was found and the campground soon spotted. It was near the pool, with its three hot tubs, kiddy pool and Olympic size

Known as the "tent man," Björgvin Holm was a member of the 1960 Icelandic Olympic team.

pond for laps. There was only one other tenant that night at the campground.

He was the most tanned Icelander I had ever seen. His grayish white hair was hidden under a woolen cap. The wind had mapped his face and he had a neatly trimmed mustache. The man wore a wool sweater, brown pants, maroon socks and a pair of sneakers with a hole at the toe in each.

He introduced himself as Björgvin Holm, better known by his Icelandic nickname — *tjaldbui.*

He was the tent man.

The tent man was 61 and said he was from Reykjavik. He was setting up his canvas tent, having unloaded it from his bicycle. Four times he had cycled the Ring Road, he said. And over the next day, I learned more.

He was a former Olympian!

Holm said he was a member of the Icelandic Olympic team which competed in Rome in 1960. His specialty was the decathlon and he finished 14th in a field of 40 athletes that year. Also, he claimed to have held the Icelandic record for the pentathlon from 1958 to 1976. He threw the javelin, did the long jump, ran 200 and 1500 meters and tossed the discus.

That was so long ago. A man interested in science, math and ideas, he said he was at the forefront of a computer revolution in Iceland, working as a computer systems analyst and getting his training in Sweden. At one point, he said he was a science writer at the largest newspaper in the country.

However, fate intervened in the form of a soured marriage. When that happened, Holm dramatically altered his lifestyle. He relinquished his possessions, and took to the road, spending half the year biking Iceland's roads. He camped out in his tent. He was given the nickname by an Icelandic television crew which did a story about him. The other half of the year he lives in a hotel.

Brilliant, eccentric were two words which came to mind. He befriended me. We took in an evening soccer game and talked over coffee in a cafe.

He had about 40 pounds of gear with him and a 10-speed bike.

"That shows you how clever I am," he said. Holm's knows that while traveling, less is more.

Music is also important to him. He says he has hidden an electric keyboard somewhere around Reykjavik, and uses it sparingly to play. He said he even composed a song for perhaps the most famous Icelandic singer in the 1990s, Bjork.

"She came to me when she was 11 and asked me to write a song. I remember it well. She had a very bright voice, even then."

Each spring, Holm buys himself a new bicycle. It's not really new, but a new used one. The summer of 1996, he was riding a blue and white

10-speed. In the winter, he works, sometimes in the fisheries. One meal a day is all he needs and when he rides, he must ride 100 kilometers a day.

Never before had a decision at a crossroads produced such a quick, obvious answer that I had taken the right road.

Holm woke the next morning filled with energy.

"Martin, bring your tape," he called out as rain tapped on my tent.

The tape recorder came along into Holm's small, circular green tent. He had me sit on a towel and take off my shoes. Taking off shoes is mandatory in Iceland and other Scandinavian countries. Before heading into pools, libraries and people's homes, it's customary to undo the shoes. There are even giant shoehorns at the pools to help put them back on.

Shoes off, a stove burned in the tent for warmth. Next to it was milk and an emptied can of peas. An opened bag of peanuts was nearby too.

As the rain pinged down upon the tent, Holm, in his cap, stayed in his sleeping bag. "Just for fun," he said and he reached into one of his two saddlebags and took out a paper he had prepared about one of his mathematical theories. It was, of course, in Icelandic. He took a square pastry from a package, called it a "cake" and used it as a prop to explain a theory about the shape of a square and its proportions as it changes sizes. I nodded politely and within minutes, my eyes glazed over. I couldn't even begin to piece together the conversation. But rather quickly, after many nods of the head and quips like "yes" or "oh yeah," we changed the subject.

Also, I learned a bit about cuisine.

I commented that he seemed to have everything he needed and I said I thought it was still fascinating that he cycled so much on only one meal a day.

He said it was a fairly big meal he would eat.

Next to the stove, he showed me some of the meat he ate.

It was a sausage.

"This is quite good," he said.

"I know. I've eaten it too."

"Are you sure?"

"It's sausage."

"Yes. But is it this sausage," he said, pointing to the name on the label.

The name, written in Icelandic, was *hrossabjogu*.

"Yeah. I've had that a couple of times."

"And what did you think?," he said, a smile starting to form around his mouth.

"A sausage is a sausage. You boil it. You eat it. It does the job."

"Do you know what this is, *hrossabjogu*?"

"A sausage."

"Do you know what kind?"

"Who cares? Parts of a cow, parts of a sheep, parts of a pig. Maybe an ear. Maybe a foot. It's sausage."

"This one is horse. Quite delicious."

I have never knowingly eaten horse before. The idea isn't repulsive to me. But it certainly must have been a surprise to me as Holm burst out in a hearty laugh as information of my culinary adventure started to be processed through my brain.

"*Yow*, quite delicious," I said, as visions of beautiful Icelandic horses filled my head.

And later that night, I checked my grocery receipts. At least twice, I had bought and eaten *hrossabjogu* during my trip.

Holm was a cycling encyclopedia.

We spoke a little while longer.

"I like this life very much. You see, I have a lot of time. As I told you, I have traveled four time around the Ring Road," he said.

"You've gone both ways," I said.

"Always in the opposite direction the next time," he answered.

"Which way is easier?"

"The wind can be a problem. I don't have in my mind which way is more difficult. I think I have had more wind against me when I go along the south coast. Last year I started the first of May and it usually takes me one month. I try to take my time. I try to cycle every day about 100 kilometers. That's not very difficult," he said.

"Have you ever gotten a ride?"

"Very seldom. I don't like it. If I have to go around Iceland, I want to go around Iceland on the bicycle, not in another vehicle. There are very few Icelanders who cycle around Iceland on a bike. Sometimes they think I am a foreigner. Once I was traveling near Egilsstadir in the east when three beautiful girls came to me, strolling by and I was on the bike. They stopped and said, 'Hello.' And 'Hello,' I said. They said, 'Oh you're an Icelander.' But they still invited me into the car for coffee. It was a very nice chat," he said.

Soon enough, it was time for me to head to the docks to catch the ferry. We cycled down and I commented on the smell of the fish plants.

"It is the smell of money," he said.

True, but what a smell.

He also solved a mystery for me.

Throughout Iceland, I had been intrigued that a culture that prides itself on its origin, its originality, had imported its stop signs from America. This is a country that sticks to its roots. It refuses to adapt its language to other languages but devised new words for modern devices from its own language.

For example, computer is *tölva*. A radio is *mtvarp*. Television is *sjonvarp*.

This truly was an independent nation.

So, this dependence on American stop signs brought a smile to my face each time I stopped at one. They were just like the red ones back home.

There, just before the ferry, we came to a stop sign.

"Why do you have stop signs in English?" I asked the tent man.

He didn't seem to understand the question and just gave me a confused look.

So I tried another question.

"How do you say 'stop' in Icelandic?"

"Stop," he said, and that smile returned.

CHAPTER NINE

Bless Iceland

The Ring Road ended where it had begun — in Reykjavik, the city by the sea. For over 850 miles, through sun, rain, hail, snow and the most ferocious of winds, it had been a test. The body had passed. The bike too, nearly. It had wounds — a broken chain, two broken clamps and a broken spoke. But wounds can be repaired.

So I made my way down to the center of the city on a Monday for Iceland's Independence Day. This island nation was having its birthday. They can throw a party in this town. The red, white and blue of the Icelandic flag flew high in the wind. Children painted their faces. They walked around on stilts, or at least tried. Cotton candy and popcorn were staples of the day. Buses flew the flag.

And when it rained so briefly, the umbrellas went up. These Icelanders are a hearty people. The strollers and carriages are outfitted for northern weather. Plastic protects the precious cargo inside. Some are wrapped in miniature sleeping bags too.

I refueled in a Chinese restaurant and upon exiting, got caught in the swarm of people and was pushed downtown in this city of cafes. I took a side street to escape. There, I saw another crowd and a sleek, black Cadillac with number one written on the license plate.

I joined the throng, that in an hour, grew to over two hundred people. We were outside the parliament building. Soon, two policemen on motorcycles flanked the Caddy. Five guards were outside the building, opening doors for people a foreigner wouldn't know. Inside was the president. Outside, there was not a gun in sight. The only weapon seen were billy clubs on the motorcycle brigade.

Each time the knob on the door would move, the cameras would automatically go to eye level. A collective sigh could be heard as the president didn't appear.

Finally, the driver starts the Caddy. Two doors opened and there she was — Vignis Finnbogadottir. Some in the crowd yell hello. The president waves. The crowd applauds. They are all just across the street. No Clint Eastwood types in sunglasses talking into their thumbs or shirtsleeves. No dog patrols. No metal detectors.

For 16 years, Finnbogadottir has held the presidency. She was elected president on June 30, 1980 and became the world's first elected woman president that day. In 1984, the people of Iceland gave her the job again. They did it again in 1988 and again in 1992. During her tenure, she was the focus of worldwide attention as Iceland hosted arms-reduction talks between the United States and the Soviet Union with Ronald Reagan and Mikhail Gorbachev sharing the stage. Finnbogadottir also hosted Pope John Paul II in June 1989 during the first visit to Iceland by a pope.

Now, Finnbogadottir was going to relinquish her office.

The handsome woman entered the car and rolled down the window. She waved and the small entourage was soon gone.

This is a country with no army. This is a country where the prisoners can go home on a holiday. The police force doesn't carry guns, as far as I could see. There is hardly a billboard outside Reykjavik. The country boasts a 100 percent literacy rate.

Yes, it has its sore points. Alcoholism is a problem. Food prices are high. The weather can warm you with a smile or beat you badly with harsh winds. But for nearly a month, many an Icelander had opened their hearts for a brief moment to let this visitor in.

On this day of celebration, once again I met members of the rescue club from Hafnarfjördur who had made me an honorary Viking for a day just a few weeks before. This time, we met in the wall-to-wall crowds of downtown and took in a few of the outdoor concerts.

And so after saying good-bye to my climbing friends, I returned to the campground next to the city pool to wait the final hours away until my early morning flight the next day.

So to Iceland, I say *bless*, but not farewell.

CHAPTER TEN

Train Through Hell

He said his name was Eric, and he was from Holland. On his back was his backpack. In his hand was a bottle of whiskey. He sat on the bench next to me in the Oslo, Norway train station and suddenly it was 1983 again.

He passed the whiskey my way. I accepted and took a swig. We were waiting. He for his northern-bound train, and me for mine. We were both tired and grungy. I took out some chocolate. He was hungry. He accepted.

The swirl of activity at the train station brought back the twirling memories to the early 1980s. Nineteen eighty-three was the year of college graduation and the seven-week American backpacking blitzkrieg through Europe with two other friends. The nights were spent sleeping in overnight trains, hostels or train station floors and benches. Bread and cheese was the standard fare.

Copious amounts of wine and beer were consumed. England, France, Switzerland, Germany, Holland, Italy, Denmark, Norway and Sweden were visited. Every young traveler had the same book, "Let's Go," and there would be a mad rush for the first place listed in the accommodation section after the train pulled into the station.

During this trip, we met an American nurse in Italy. She was living in a small Swiss town and rolled out the welcome mat. We made sure we passed through that town to stay at her place. What made it more amazing was that the day after we arrived, she headed out and left us there alone for a few days. We were strangers, and she left us the keys. The only proviso was that we didn't eat the crunchy peanut butter.

"That's expensive around here," I remember her saying.

That was the year of sleeping under the Leaning Tower of Pisa, of hanging out in the cafes of Amsterdam, of seeing great pieces of art and architecture, and of learning that bottles of beer can be opened with more than a bottle opener. The trip was a whirlwind and an eye opener to different ways of doing things.

The whiskey in the bottle was receding. The Dutch backpacker told his story, of how he just outsmarted border authorities. He had been searched for marijuana. He was a bit incredulous as to authorities searching a 19-year-old for marijuana just because he was from a country with relaxed cannabis laws. Of course, he was carrying the weed and when he was being searched he just held the two grams in his hand. The authorities went through his backpack, and had trouble stuffing his sleeping bag back into the sack. They asked for his assistance. He complied, and during the re-stuffing of the bag, added the two grams to the sack's contents.

Soon enough, the Dutchman left to get his train, and I was alone to watch the world in the train station.

Waiting is a skill a traveler should learn well. It is inevitable. The waiting began back in Iceland the morning of June 19. The plane was slated for an early morning take-off. There was a three hour delay. So, one reads, talks a little and waits.

The airline made an announcement that passengers could get a free breakfast, and there was a dash for the restaurant and more open-faced sandwiches. To the American, an open-faced sandwich can be a shock as we are used to two slices of bread. This isn't the case in Europe. One slice is standard. I quickly got over it.

The flight to Oslo was uneventful, as was Norwegian customs. A bus took all the gear to the train station. Bicycles on trains are allowed. But, the bike must go on the night train on long journeys.

The bicycle was checked, albeit with some trepidation, and given into the capable hands of the Norwegian State Railway. My rig did not have to be dismantled, though any accessories like pump, water bottle and handlebar bag had to be taken off. The packaging of the bike on the flight over was similar. Icelandair had huge rollers with plastic bags. Just stick the bike in the bag and roll it over to an attendant.

The train left close to midnight. I settled in for the 17 hour, nearly 1,000 mile journey to Bodø, above the Arctic Circle.

Sometime during the night, as I slept in my oblivious whiskey stupor, a landslide occurred a few hundred miles up on the train's route. This was so far away, but it would have an impact. People died. Homes were destroyed. Roads were covered in mud and the train line was swept over.

It was a restless night, tossing in the sleeper car on a pull-out seat. I brushed my teeth at least twice to try and get rid of the foul, cotton mouth taste, but still, twice wasn't enough.

Feeling more taut than the propeller on a thin, balsam model airplane, it was a welcome feeling to switch trains at Trondheim in the morning and stretch the miles from my legs. The thrill was having breakfast — a soda and a hot dog for about $5.

The train left at 8:30 a.m. for the remaining 453-mile leg to Bodø. This was a truly stunning ride. The train seemed to be floating on the edge of clear waters. The green, how vibrant against the memories of a rugged, wild Iceland, was most pronounced in the tall, thin evergreens. Green meadows hosted horses. The reds, whites and greens of the homes stood out amongst the landscape. The coast was left behind and the mountains came into play. Clear blue lakes, rushing rivers and snow-capped mountains were seen through bleary and weary eyes. Trees gave way to nothingness as we climbed. Trees, there were trees. You don't realize how much you miss trees until you visit Iceland, where most of the landscape is devoid of them. It was easy to get lost in nature's movie.

The four tones from the loudspeaker roused me from a daydream. Due to a problem ahead — it was not disclosed what the problem was in English — we would have to get off the train at Trofors and use buses to Moi i Rana.

This didn't phase me at all. I just figured the workers would take the checked in luggage, my bike and body bag, on the buses and they would catch up with me. The crowd rushed to the two buses, packing them immediately. The overflow took a taxi.

I noticed two other cyclists with their bikes in a heated conversation, in English, with the scurrying attendants. The railway workers weren't letting the bikes on the bus. There was no room, they said. The bikers were insistent. The bikes were going onto the bus, they argued.

The bikers won the battle. The two bicycles went in the compartment under the bus.

I looked in there. It was packed.

I had a bike too.

I asked a frazzled worker about my bike.

"There is no room. It will come later," he said.

Trepidation started its walk through my mind. But this time, didn't get far. Sometimes you just have to let people do their job. There appeared to be order in the frenzy.

I left my bicycle with them, taking the computer, and one saddlebag with necessary items and a sleeping bag.

I grabbed a seat next to a guy with long, straight blonde hair tied in a pony tail. He had a bushy beard and had the look of a liberal, human rights activist.

Turned out, he was.

Instead of going into the army, which is a one-year mandatory sentence for Norwegian men, he told me, he was able to spend 16 months in "civil service," working with the mentally disabled.

The man acted as a translator, telling me about the landslide and updating me on the announcements the bus driver was making.

The serpentine road was narrow, and soon I would fall asleep. I was awakened when the bus driver pulled over at an inn for a rest stop.

I followed the flock into the inn. They were selling chocolate, ice cream and soda.

I got a soda and chocolate and gave the guy a 50 when he said the cost was 27.

I went back to the bus and sat next to the bushy beard.

"Did they take your kronor?" he asked.

"Of course. Why wouldn't they?"

"We're in Sweden."

"Huh."

"Part of the bus ride goes to Sweden and then back into Norway," he said.

I got out a map and he showed me.

"Maybe they gave you your change in Swedish kronor," he said.

I dug into my pants pockets and held out the coins. I wasn't familiar with the coins and spread them out.

The bushy beard took a quick look and said, "No, they are all from Norway."

So, border crossings are easy in northern Scandinavia. We didn't even have to stop, I was told.

Nor did we have to stop crossing back into Norway and Moi i Rana where a train was waiting.

We played a game of musical chairs once again. We said good-bye to the bus and hello to the train.

I settled into my seat and listened to my rumbling tummy. Funny, I thought, had this been America, we probably would have received some sort of refreshment for our inconvenience. An announcement came over the speaker on the train. A few people got up from their seats.

Then another announcement was made, and more people headed to another car.

It came again and more people left.

I finally asked someone what was going on.

I was told they were serving free coffee and sandwiches in the dining car.

I joined the movement and then went back to my seat.

We finally crossed the Arctic Circle at 7:10 p.m. I saw the bleak, treeless gray. There was snow and rushing water. Cairns were on the right side of the train. I could see the tourism booth by the road, put right on the circle as a dividing line. I saw the northern nothingness. Rocks, sand, snow. Would I be able to spend the whole summer here? From the safety of a rail car it looked so peaceful. I couldn't feel the cold, nor the rain, nor the snow, nor the wind, nor any other element that might be right outside the window.

As I wondered, the landscape changed as we descended into a valley. The green returned. Blue skies opened up. Trees and jagged peaks returned.

The train pulled into Bodø about two and a half hours late. I was told my bike would be coming the next day. It was night, but the sun was still high. The hostel was on the upper floor of the train station. I checked in and roomed with an Australian backpacker who asked about the trip.

I told him my saga.

"Sounds like it was a trip through hell," he said.

"Something like that," I replied.

He appeared to be waiting for some sort of reaction from me. It didn't come. He took out a map and showed me where the train had gone.

Outside of Trondheim, there is a town through which the train passes. It's called Hell.

CHAPTER ELEVEN

A Summer
Night's Ride

In Norwegian, å means "little creek." Å, pronounced "oh," is also a tiny fishing village on the south end of the island Moskenes in the enchanted Lofoten Islands. Enchanted, that is, when the weather cooperates.

The islands make up an archipelago to the west of Norway's mainland, above the Arctic Circle. The islands consist of mountains and peaks, wide open ocean, sheltered inlets and sheep grazing the steep inclines. About 24,500 people live on the seven principal islands of Lofoten which are linked by boats, bridges and tunnels.

Northern Norway's Arctic coast is blessed by the warm winds of the Gulf Stream. This enables Arctic tulips to grow and temperatures to reach the mid-50s and low-60s. When the sun is out, one needs to look no further for a taste of Eden. When it's not, have a raincoat handy.

The islands, which are laid out like pearls on a string, are a few hours west by ferry from Bodø, a city of 40,000. The sun was shining that first day of summer. Life was teaming in the downtown mall. Beer flowed. Cigarettes were smoked. The flock sat at outdoor cafes. Merchants sold their goods.

They were celebrating the longest day of the year.

I was celebrating being re-united with my bicycle. As promised, it had been delivered. Now it was time for the ferry to the Lofotens where I would spend four days and start the ride north to the top of Europe.

The first people came to Lofoten about 6,000 years ago, surviving on fishing and hunting. Though much of the deer, bear, reindeer, lynx and beaver are gone, the fishing remains. Just inhale deeply by any of the fishing hamlets. That is the smell of stockfish.

Wooden racks of drying fish are a familiar sight. Cod from the Barents Sea come to the Lofoten area to spawn. Fishermen catch the fish and haul them back to shore in their boats. The fish are hung out to dry just like in Iceland. But instead of butter, the Norwegians suggest the fish be consumed with a beer. Maybe two.

The fish and the smell are constant reminders of what the islanders have had to face in their years on Lofoten. Before television, the computer and radio, families would gather in their red and yellow fishing cabins after a day on the water, mending nets, churning butter or knitting sweaters. They would tell stories in the dark, chill of winter. One story that would be told was that of the "Voice of the Sea".

There once lived a boy who used to play practical jokes on the fishermen. He would swim out to the fishing boats in the sea, or stow a ride, and then pretend he was drowning. The fishermen would then have to pull him up into the boat. Of course, the boy would be very cold and he would stand on the deck afterwards and see if the fishermen would warm him up by offering him their sweater or hats or gloves.

If the fishermen relinquished the sweater and things, it was said they would be rewarded from that day on by having the wind at their back, lots of fish in their nets and would be warned of foul weather ahead. If the fishermen did nothing, they would perish.

The boy was nature, the voice of the sea. The lesson to be learned was one of preparedness.

The ferry made stops at Røst, a somewhat flat island known for its population of puffins, and Værøy, with its jagged green-gray mighty cliffs. At one time, hunters used to catch eagles bare-handed here. But that is no more.

The ferry continued on to Moskenes.

It was approaching midnight as the boat neared the dock. I still couldn't see the midnight sun. Though it was as light as mid-day, the sun was hidden behind the clouds. This would be a common phenomenon. I would not actually see the midnight sun until early July, when I got up in the middle of the night to relieve myself. It didn't occur to me until the next morning that I finally had seen the sun.

The sun was hiding. The golden orb hid behind the peaks. The mountains lost their definition in the flat light. Instead of seeming full and vibrant, they appeared as though someone had made a black paper silhouette. They had used scissors to cut the razor-sharp peaks.

Moskenes was quiet when the boat pulled in. There was the initial excitement of the passengers disembarking. Cars met a few of them. Others took a taxi to who knows where.

The signs indicated the way to Å. After eight hours on a boat, lounging on a deck chair and exchanging chitchat in strange English, the muscles called out to be used. It was only a couple of easy miles to the tip of the island and a campground.

Most of those who lived in the villages were asleep. An occasional walker shared the road. The salt air was like perfume, the perfect compliment for a visual meal of homes on stilts, fish racks, peaks and tiny storybook red houses.

The rhythm of bicycle and rider cut the silence. A television was playing. The road rolled in the folds of the landscape. A dormant snowplow foretold of heavy snows in winter. Boats stayed in their slips. Birds clacked in the towering cliffs.

The sign said Å, and I laughed out loud. Here I was, alone, on the southernmost point of an Arctic island. The road ended just past the first of what was to be several long, dark and dank Norwegian tunnels. Here, was the end of the road. Or, a beginning. All one had to do was turn around and the end becomes a start.

Other people were out on the rocks at land's end, gazing out into the calm waters on a mid-summer's night. This wasn't a dream. This was real.

Gulls echoed against the towering cliffs. In my mind I saw climbers, hooking in their carabineers and using their ropes to scale these rocks near the top of the world. Straddling the bike, I could hear the water lap the rocks, the hum of a distant motor, the chattering of a foreign language and the serenity in my heart.

Land's end had a campground and long after midnight, sleep came in the Arctic night.

Not only does John Molid, 39, run the campground in Å, in the winter, he's the plow guy. Though the Gulf Stream does produce a warming effect, winters are still quite cold and drifting snow can cause the snow to pile up high. He plows about five miles of backroads between Å and Moskenes. For 20 years, he used to drive the area ambulance which once was owned by his father.

"Last year I was taking away snow in October," he said, collecting

The Norwegian coastline is a never-ending postcard of jagged peaks, fish racks and red fishing shacks called rorbeuers.

my fee for the night before. At times, storms can dump six feet in one stretch. He has lived in Å all of his life.

"Everyone knows everyone," he said. "That can be bad. But it can also be good. We know all the bad people."

As for the name Å, he said it means a small river.

"It's the shortest name in the world for a town, I think," he said.

The snow falls can be long, and deep.

"Some days I work the whole day and night. I take one road, finish it and then have to go back and do it again."

Every summer, he says, the tourists come and ask about the origins of Å and every summer he explains.

As for eating fish, "Sometimes I get tired of fish. The people here, if you can't have fish once a week, you feel it. It is in my blood. I think maybe it was the first meal I had as a kid."

Though small, Å has two museums, a restaurant, store and a post office. The nearest bank isn't far, just a mile away. Some 170 people live there.

Travelers can rent a fishing shack called a *rorbuer* for a night as an alternative means of accommodation on the Lofotens.

One *rorbuer* at Stamsund is a budget-traveler's dream. Roar Justad has been running it as a hostel for 22 years. With its waterfront location and warming woodstoves inside, visitors often spend longer there than they had planned. Justad also loans hostelers his fishing gear and will charter fishing trips. Frequently, visitors will share the day's catch, grilling or cooking it up in tin foil with butter and lemon juice.

Travelers seem to be drawn to certain restaurants, bars and hostels throughout the world. In 1987, to sleep on the beaches of Eilat, Israel and see the shorelines and hills of Jordan, Egypt and Saudi Arabia was raved about by fellow travelers. In 1983, backpack rats were heading to the Milky Way in Amsterdam and the Hofbrau House in Munich, Germany for nocturnal beverage and fun.

Those traveling through the Lofoten Islands in the summer of 1996 had Justad's hostel. There's the song "Hotel California" by the Eagles, which has the line, "You can check out anytime, but you can never leave."

For some, the hostel had similar appeal.

On the harbor, the Stamsund hostel is supposedly the hostel of dreams.

It is laid back. Justad's boat is anchored at the dock. Row boats can be chartered for free. Blocks and knives for cutting fish are on the deck. If there is sun, the mountains can be seen.

Why was the place popular? That can be hard to answer. The hostel had a coolness about it. Maybe it came from Justad himself. He had jet black hair and a scruffy, low-rent look to him. But he was king in a low-budget utopia. Ask him why the hostel is a mecca, he talks about fish.

"When there is fishing, people share," he said. "When one person shares, then everyone shares. In the city, it is not usual for sharing. When you have fish for free, people share and that makes contact."

There it is. Fish will make you free.

The hostel was crowded and accommodations were a not-so-clean looking mattress on the floor of a co-ed room on the second floor. This was 1983 again. Was this something a 34-year-old college-educated man was supposed to be doing? Who cares? This was living.

There was a celebration going on, a belated mid-summer's eve barbecue, with grilled fish and bottles of white wine being passed around. But even before the party got going, the attraction was the indoor kitchen

Hostels, like this one in Stamsund, brought back memories of backpacking through Europe.

table.

The picnic-style table was a magnet for travelers. One person leaves, and another fills the place, any time of day. The melange of language made rounds. Pick a country and maybe it was there. South Korea was across from France which was next to New Zealand which passed the salt to Germany which got up to get water for Belgium which was eyeing Australia which sat right next to America.

Each person representing his or her country was also something of a stereotype. The British sipped their tea. The Australians had their vegemite spread. The French longed for their bread of home.

The strangers shared. They exchanged coffee and tea. The vodka was passed around. Travel tips were given. Go here. Forget there. It's cheap here. It's expensive there.

They speak English. They speak their native tongues with their brethren. Those who master more than one tongue flip flop between countries.

One backpacker told a story of speaking English to other travelers on the train. A couple, not speaking English, started to talk about the young travelers, saying how dirty they were, and how cheap they were. The English speakers babbled on.

Before they left the train, they made a point of wishing the couple well, in the language the man and woman had been speaking.

From the kitchen table, the festivities moved outside to the deck, and later, back inside to the kitchen which had now become a night club. Two guitarists and a flutist took the impromptu stage. The three were travelers, on their own trips. Neil Young songs were played. They segued into a bit of ZZ Top. What's a kitchen concert without Zeppelin's "Stairway to Heaven?"

What made this magic? What makes total strangers get together and share a kitchen, a drink, a bathroom and even a bedroom? They really share and open their hearts to people, chances are, they will never see again. It wasn't just young people. Families were there too.

Why can this happen? Is it because people are on vacation? Are they playing out roles for themselves, inventing themselves anew far from home? Maybe leaving the stresses of the "real world" behind makes them open up. Maybe it's that they are traveling, and realize it's all about sharing. It's knowing that for the moment, there is no other place than right where you are. You are there because you want to be. No one has forced you to be there. For the moment, the hostel is your home. Those around you, for whatever time period, are your friends and family.

Hostels also make you wonder. Friendships and acquaintances sometimes last for hours and maybe even days and months if you hook up with the right person. But also, there are times you meet a traveler and you wonder what if? What if I spent more time with this person. Would this person become my friend, my lover? What if?

There are people who pass much too quickly through your life. You write your thoughts in your diary. The people are fresh in your mind as the journey continues and even back home as you spin your tales again and again for those with envy in their eyes. But then the photos get put away. "Real world" life returns. Work returns. The memories fade, until, if you are lucky, another trip begins.

As the familiar songs were played, thoughts drifted back to places and people visited. Whatever happened to the two Belgian bicyclists I met in Alaska in 1994 who were cycling around the world? Whatever happened to the hitchhiker I met in 1979 during a cross-country bicycle ride who handed out a business card that thanked people for the ride? What became of the girls from Minnesota, or was it Wisconsin, who stopped by the campground during that very same trip?

What happens to the people we meet? Why do we meet?

Perhaps is it just to meet. To keep the trips going. To make sure the road is well-traveled and laughter is heard and stories are told. It's to share a good beer, a smile and a pat on the shoulder when the road isn't as smooth as was envisioned.

CHAPTER TWELVE

Cold Inside,
Cold Outside

"How do I know there is a midnight sun when there is no sun?" This was a question scrawled in English on the wall of a rundown shack by the side of a road. I wasn't the first traveler to seek it for shelter from the rain. There were other observations in there too.

If the graffiti was to be believed, the shack had been a haven for travelers since 1971. That was the date of the earliest scrawl. The latest was 1989. The writings were in Finnish, Italian, English and Spanish.

"*Hay muchos mosquitos*," wrote one visitor.

The most provocative musing came from New Zealand and the felt tip pen of a Brian Edward Beard, born 1945, and late of Wellington, New Zealand. He wrote: "*Norge*, your country is magnificent and your women .are beautiful but hitch-hiking in Nordland in your 'summer' weather is like swimming up shit creek with both hands tied beneath your back."

The day dawned cold and rainy. Actually, most days dawned this way. The sun made rare appearances, and when it did, the Arctic blue and green sparkled.

When it didn't, Norway was dubbed the Land of the Midnight Rain, or the Land of the Midnight Herring. And when it rained, any roof became a castle.

Dampness spawns colds. Cycling with a cold is not fun. You are asking your body to make a choice. Should the body fight the little bacteria buggers that are filling the nooks and crannies with mucous, and making the yellow stuff flow out of the nose and onto both gloves in a disgusting, rhythmic drip or does the body flow the energy to the legs to pedal the miles?

Clearly, the war within was felt. Coughing shouted at the morning. A runny nose does not make for pleasant cycling. My voice was frog-like.

Leaving the Lofotens, the route ran through regions of northern Norway called Nordland, then Troms and finally Finnmark. Often the roads would end. A ferry would be waiting. Travelers would cross the water, disembark, and continue on another road. These areas would be my home for the next several weeks, with occasional roadside snapshots filling the days. These were brief, though memorable encounters, not far from the shoulder of the narrow, hilly road.

Even though the sun was playing a game of hide and seek, it could not conceal the spectacular scenery of a land whose name translates to "way north." If Iceland was rugged and wild, Norway was like a polished stone, rich in quality from every angle.

The fjords, with their toppings of snow, were magnificent against the sea. Long bridges over fast-moving rivers called for a pause to take in the mountains that hit the sky.

Even with a cold, a certain giddiness would come for a visit during a lunch stop with foods like mackerel in tomato sauce, flat bread and peanuts. During one such moment, about 40 miles south of Narvik, the northernmost stop during the winter World Cup ski tour, I was roused from my trance by a fellow cyclist.

He spoke no English.

I spoke no German.

But this didn't stop him from telling me about his trip.

I wish I had recorded the actual conversation. Nonetheless, I did a lot of nodding as he told me he was cycling from Germany up to the North Cape and then back down somewhere. I wasn't really sure where that somewhere was.

He was a peculiar looking man, but what biker isn't? His right pant leg was rolled up to prevent the cuff from being digested by the chain. He only carried two small saddlebags and a handlebar bag. He had a camping mat and a spare tire on the back of the bike.

A scruffy gray beard covered his chin and glasses were perched on his nose. The hood of his windbreaker was pulled tightly over his head, and was covered by a helmet too.

He wanted to know where I was from and I thought I made it clear I had flown from Boston and that I first went to Iceland, but I guess that didn't come through. He went to his bike (a nice, expensive American one) and brought out a map and guidebook of Norway.

We opened the map and I showed him Iceland and then he understood I was an American. He had pointed to England, apparently thinking I was British. He wanted to know how many kilometers the ride around Iceland was and how many days it took me. Then he wanted to see my route in Norway. I showed him where I took the plane, ferry, and train to get to where we were having this quasi-conversation. He didn't seem impressed with my taking all this alternative transportation and wanted to know how many kilometers I had ridden all together.

Well, he was going to make sure he told me about how many kilometers he had ridden. Back into the handlebar bag he went and out came his diary. Though I don't remember where he started or where he was ending up, he took me page by page of his trip, saying where he started that day, where he ended, what the weather was like and how much distance he had traveled.

He went through the first day, then the second day and then the third day.

It was the same thing. He told me the place he started, the place he ended, the weather and the distance.

He went on to the fourth day, the fifth day, the sixth day.

The frog in my throat started to jump. He had his cadence, I started getting mine, coughing as he relayed his adventure.

The seventh day, eighth day, ninth day.

Cough. Cough. Cough.

Day ten. Day eleven.

Cough. An "excuse me". Slight body spasm.

Day twelve. Day thirteen.

Convulsion city.

Day fourteen.

"Vitamins," he says.

Day fifteen. Day sixteen.

Vitamins, he says. He went through all 26 days and over 3,000 kilometers of his trip and the only word he could say to me was vitamins.

Did he have any? If so, he didn't offer. He just wrapped up his things, shook my gloved hand, and hit the road.

The "vitamin man" was history.

The mountains were gone. They would be there for a moment. But the fog and the drizzle would hide them. This far north, even in late June,

The author takes a break by the side of the road with the rugged peaks of Norway in the background.

a touch of winter seemed to hold on.

The day called out for a fire. Instead of riding, time could be spent in front of a fireplace or woodstove, in a log cabin. There would be warmth. There would be a smoky fragrance.

But these were just the thoughts of a lone rider, going slowly in a cold-induced, both within and outside, misery.

Though the cabin did not materialize, a teepee did. It wasn't actually a teepee like Native Americans in North America used. The tent up ahead was similar. But it was not the same.

Smoke was rising from the tent. Though in this part of the world, northern Norway, the tent is called something else — a kåta. It is a simple and practical tent used by one of the oldest people you'll find at the top the world. They are the Sami.

The Sami are northern Scandinavia's indigenous people. They have their own flag, their own anthem, language, culture, identity and customs. About 70,000 of them live in an area known as Lapland, which is a land that stretches across the top of Norway, Sweden, Finland and Russia.

Thousands of years ago, the Sami herded reindeer, fished and hunted. Time marched on, and livelihoods changed. The Sami were chased from their homeland as the various countries were settled. Now, they are an ethnic minority.

Their handicrafts with distinctive designs and decorations are sold throughout the region. Their oral tradition has been passed down through tales and a form of songs called *yoiking*. Their literature, theater and visual arts continue.

Though a small percentage of Sami make their living from reindeer herding now, they live throughout the four countries, and at least in Scandinavia, set up shop by the roadside to sell knives, reindeer antlers, skins, dolls, hats and clothing. The colors of the Sami are blue, red, yellow and green. Many of the elders wore traditional clothing with these colors, down to pointed elf-like boots.

They sit by the roadside, and wait for customers. They shop in the towns in modern supermarkets. They drive cars.

They exist.

And along the E-6, they would set up their tents and do business.

The Sami tent was a rest area cafe. This was where the smoke and a delicious smell was emanating from. Inside the tent, was a place to eat. The warmth was welcome.

The tent was large, with stumps of birch wood to sit upon. There were animal skin covers as padding. In the middle of the cafe was a fire with kettles and a simmering cauldron. Hot chocolate, tea and coffee were all offered, but there was this stew-like smell coming from the black pot. Other customers were ordering it, being given a plastic cup and then dipping a ladle into the creation and being rejuvenated by its taste and warmth.

When in a roadside tent, one follows the motions of others.

The concoction took the chill from the body's insides. The fire did the same. The soup was consumed, slowly. It was tasty, somewhat gamy, yet pleasing.

So good, another cup was had.

Rested, and warm, it was time to leave.

The young Sami girl, dressed in traditional colors behind the counter, was asked a question.

"By the way, what kind of soup was that?"

"Reindeer," she said.

CHAPTER THIRTEEN

Fifty Years On The River

For most of his 70 years, Håkon Hansen has lived along northern Norway's Reisa River. From the windows of the house he built in 1969, which he constructed only after the other house he built burned down, you can see the river which now must run through his veins.

The river has been Hansen's teacher and has taught him much. What it has taught him is personal, and even though he speaks Norwegian, Swedish, Finnish, German and Sami, it is hard to convey the lessons to a stranger through an interpreter.

Hansen is well-known throughout the Reisa valley. The summer of 1996 marked his 50th year of piloting the 30 foot-long river boats he makes down the river to the Reisa National Park. He takes hikers who want to trek the 70 miles or so to the Norwegian Sami capital of Kautokeino from the park's border, or tourists who want to see Mollisfossen, one of Europe's highest waterfalls — over 1,000 feet high. Or, he'll just take them fishing for salmon.

The salmon do bite in the Reisa. One such fish weighed in at nearly 70 pounds in 1922, landing it in a nearby Tromsø museum. But for Hansen, the biggest fish he caught was about five or six years ago.

On the living room wall, near the antlers and skins of other trophies, is a color photo of Hansen, a bespectacled, strong, outdoorsman, father and husband, with a salmon tipping the scales at some 40 pounds. He remembers that day, sitting in a boat by himself. The salmon was hooked

*Guide Håkon Hansen makes his own sleds out of wood and bends the
runners during the summer.*

and then it felt as if the salmon was pulling the boat for 500 yards. He
tried reeling it in, letting out line, reeling it in and using the line as a
brake. But the big fish kept going. Finally, both fish and fisherman were
exhausted after the fight and in silent waters, the salmon stopped. Hansen
landed the salmon into the boat.

Fish is plentiful here. Why just the other night, Hansen went down to
the harbor near here and caught more than 100 fish. Some he freezes.
Some he smokes. Some are marinated in sugar and salt.

Aside from the fish, there are moose too. When the tourists and mosquitoes are gone by autumn and the snows arrive, soon the river freezes.
The temperature dips below zero and stays there until it feels like leaving.
The boats are put away and the snow machine takes over. Not only does
Hansen make his boats from the birch wood in the forest around him, but
he makes sleds for snowmobiles. Wood is everywhere. Five years worth
of firewood is stacked, he says. That way if he ever gets sick, there will
still be heat. He takes a walk outside his house and seems immune to the
mosquitoes. There, he displays the rungs of the sled he must mold in the
summer. In the winter, he finishes the sleds, about 10 feet long.

And when the Reisa is frozen and the snow is high upon the house he
shares with his wife Margit, Hansen rides the river on his machine. It was
on one day, he almost met death. How cold it was, he couldn't say. Bone-
chilling it was and Hansen was alone, zipping down the winter highway.

He couldn't see much as a whiteout blocked his way. Suddenly, he saw seven figures ahead. He couldn't stop. The seven were moose and they scampered away. One choose a unique route and jumped right over Hansen's head as he sped by. Had the animal missed, Hansen believes he would have been killed.

Hansen's life is one of survival and resourcefulness. During the "war," which World War II is referred to in northern Norway, the Germans had a prison camp in the area for deserters. It was in the camp where Hansen learned his German, playing cards with soldiers, deserters and officers. He learned his Swedish a few years later when his family emigrated to Sweden for 27 months so they wouldn't have to work for the Germans. They later returned.

Hansen is a man who knows his river, each rock, each island, each change that comes with melting snow. He has been there when a spooked moose nearly jumped into the boat, startling tourists. He has been there when he and a tourist father pulled off the father's children's boots to put out a fire Hansen spotted in the woods from his boat.

He is a person one meets for a few hours and relishes over a lifetime.

CHAPTER FOURTEEN

Where The Wild Things Roam

The fire was already roaring inside the wooden-style yurt. Roger Dahl, Norwegian sled dog driver, had coffee and cake prepared. Reindeer skins lined the circular tent, providing warmth and a cushion.

"Here," he said, "this might mean something to you to, being on a bicycle."

It was a coffee mug with an inscription that read: "I've spent many nights at peace with myself...alone with my dogs. It is at these times when I remember who and what is important to me, when thoughts come most clear...and memories are made."

Dahl has lots of memories and Finnmark is a place that helps make them. This is a region that is as far north as you can get in Norway. Mountains, fjords, valleys, rivers and plains create the landscape. It is home to the Alta River, where 20 pound salmon are common and wealthy Americans and Germans cast their fly-rods under the midnight sun, paying upwards of $10,000 a week for the privilege. In these parts, there is a tradition. When fishermen catch a salmon, they drink cognac in celebration. They also pour some in the salmon's mouth. As someone said to me, we may not always catch salmon, but we do catch cognac all the time.

Like many in these parts, the wild outdoors has called to Dahl through the pages of Jack London's classics and the incredible Arctic expeditions of Norwegians Roald Amundsen and Fridtjof Nansen. A policeman for over 20 years, he left his beat in 1995 and started his own kennel and outfitting company in Alta called Canyon Huskies, providing sled dog demonstrations and hikes in the summer and dog sled rides in the winter. He was one of two Norwegian racers in the 1996 Iditarod sled dog race, coming in 19th among the 61 competitors. Actually, he was the last racer out of the gate and nearly took home Rookie of the Year honors, but an Alaskan zoomed past him during the last 25 miles.

Whether bicycling or driving a dog team in winter, Finnmark is a place where stories abound. Dahl remembers one adventure when he and another driver were out with six tourists, three in each sled. They passed a moose laying down in the snow. Dahl knew the moose would start plotting something for when the two teams returned. Dahl's sled passed by, uneventful, but soon the still winter was filled with chaos. The second team somehow started a battle with the moose, the dogs tipping the moose over. Dahl went to help and then after all escaped uninjured, spent the next two hours untangling the 20 dogs!

Dahl entered his first dog sled race in 1983, and it was nine years later that he won a prestigious European race, the Finnmarkslopet, a 650 mile loop in the very region Dahl calls home.

Talk to a musher and when they speak of their dogs, it's like they are talking about their children, their brother, their friend. There is a bond between driver and dog.

In 1993, Dahl was out with his dog team in a brutal storm. The blizzard roared and visibility was non-existent. He had lost the trail markers. Instead of plowing ahead, he decided to wait it out. He dug a snow shelter and there driver and dogs didn't move for 12 hours. The weather calmed. Dahl couldn't get his bearings. He left that to his dogs. Though Dahl didn't know where he was, he trusted the dogs to lead the way. They did, eventually picking up the trail once again, and finding home.

"Whatever you do, the dogs are there for you," he said in between cigarettes. He had a bandaged hand that he had cut splitting firewood just days before. "A person who doesn't work with dogs, can't see it. I can see what is in their minds. If I want to go to one place, I think it, and the dogs go there without telling me. I think they can read my mind."

A few miles from Dahl's house is where Eli Jensen lives. She's also a musher, but not in the competitive sense. She enjoys raising her Alaskan huskies as a lifestyle. Trained electrician, part-time student, she drove her first dog team in 1977 at age 12.

"You must be willing to live with dogs all the time. It's a lifestyle, not a hobby," she said.

The yelping of the dogs fills the backyard, not far from the sea where just the night before, she and her friend, Torbjorn Kristiansen, spent a few hours fishing and landed about 160 coalfish. Yes, if Norway has something, it's plenty of fish, water and ever-changing weather. There are no fishing limits either for residents, they say.

Jensen, with ever-present coffee and rolling her own cigarettes, comes back with a photo album and shows women mushers in what is becoming an annual event in Finnmark. For one weekend in April, the women have their own race, traveling some 80 miles over three days, talking, joking, drinking and running naked from the river after taking part in the steamy saunas. The race is called the Aasgaardsreia.

In the winter-like spring of 1996, 55 women competed. Usually, Jensen explained, the women have helped their husbands or boyfriends handle the dog teams, but don't drive. This is an opportunity for camaraderie and fun. Plus, drinking.

"The men show up and try and tell us what to do. Do that. Don't do that. But we are not interested in the men. We are interested in the dogs," she says with a laugh.

In winter, mushers can drive on the frozen Alta River. But in summer, the waters are prime salmon fishing.

Those not fishing can take a ride on a 30 foot riverboat into the Sautso Canyon, the largest canyon in Northern Europe.

Tor Kjetil Wisløff is at the control of the wooden boat. His family has been guiding visitors on the river for over 100 years and now runs a sports center called Alta Friluftspark. The boat slices against the current. The gulls above scan the waters for fish below. Ducks fly across the sky. When Wisløff cuts the engine and silence reigns, soon the sounds of salmon jumping make one want to grab a fishing line and join the hunt. Long, thin waterfalls empty into the river from snow still hanging onto winter. The steep cliffs are painted green with the leaves of the birch tree. Wisløff has been guiding now for some 21 years.

"My father taught me to drive a boat when I was eight years old," he said. "My father taught me to fish. So the father must teach the son. I have a son, nine years old and it is time I teach him to drive the boat."

And when he does, perhaps Wisløff's son will add to the stories spun in reaches of the Far North.

The path to this strange and wonderful time in Alta began with a July 4th snowball.

At least that's how I want to think it started.

Maybe it happened as I cycled through the mountains of Gildetun, stopping to throw a few snowballs on a July summer day. Maybe it happened while on that same day I though how great it would be to go to a barbecue and watch an Independence Day parade. See the stars and stripes go by. Listen to talk about how the Red Sox would disappoint the faithful again at the end of the season. But this wouldn't happen on this holiday because it wasn't a day of celebration at the top of the world.

It wasn't until a day later, that I learned my grandmother had died on Independence Day.

The news came during a roadside phone call in the small town of Talvik. I had stopped to check in with the significant other back in New Hampshire and she told me the news. I then tried to get hold of my parents, but there was no answer.

The news didn't come as a surprise, nor a shock. It wasn't until a few miles later, that the reality sunk in and I started crying. With no one to offer comfort, with no familiar shoulder nearby, with no one to hear my memories, all I could do was ride.

She was 87 and had lived a good life. But it was knowing that I would never hear her stories again, the stories peppered with words from another land and era that I didn't know, that carried the most sadness. She had a way of telling a story that involved postscripts throughout. Instead of saying something like, "and so on," she would say, "P.S." Just like you write at the end of a letter.

Grandma Hannah wasn't well. This we knew before the trip. The last time I saw her was in May prior to going on the journey. Her ability to still laugh, to still make light of her failing health, brought smiles to those around her, even though physically, one could sense the end was near.

My parents and I had talked about what could be inevitable over the next few months — her death. If she died while I was overseas, I would not attend the funeral. However, I would attend a service at a later date upon my return.

Through her death, one realizes how life marches on, regardless of where all the participants in one's particular world happened to be. When you travel, you are not immune to news from back home. Back home does not stand still, just as the traveler does not. Events go on. People age, get sick, get well, fall in love, break up, get jobs, fix homes, are born and die. Life isn't put on hold. Life goes on.

So when I finally got into Alta, a thriving town with ancient rock carvings at its museum and a jumping off place for adventure, I headed to the first payphones I saw to try and call my parents. We talked. We reminisced. We decided on an e-mail eulogy to be read at the funeral.

Across from the phones was the local visitor information center. There, I introduced myself and showed one of the workers a copy of an article about me that had run in the country's largest newspaper a few days before. A journalist in Tromsø — a jewel of a city with its huge spanning bridge, walking streets, cafes, polar museum and referred to as the "Paris of the north" — had done an interview with me. I figured it would be easier to show, instead of tell.

I just told her I had something to type and wondered if I could use the phone to hook up to the Internet.

It wasn't a problem, said the employee, Siw Elin Wideborg.

There in the office, as memories were visited, I wrote the eulogy and then sent it electronically to my parent's home. There, it was printed out, and later read at the funeral.

I thanked Wideborg for her kindness. Then I learned that while I had been writing, she had been planning.

Coincidentially, there were two representatives from the regional tourism association in the office and all three had been putting together an itinerary for me to see the area, complete with guide.

So, over the next two days, I was whisked around Alta, which is how I met people like Roger Dahl, Eli Jensen and and Tor Kjetil Wisløff.

That night, Wideborg picked me up at the campground I was staying, and took me to dinner at a restaurant, Altastua, which had just opened the month before.

Casual elegance and bicycle clothing met head on in the candle light which flickered against the light Norwegian wood. One of the dining areas was an actual cabin that had been moved there from the local slate mine which I was to visit after dinner. For several weeks, my diet had been pasta with tuna, pasta with mackeral and pasta with pasta. This restaurant served cuisine from reindeer to salmon.

My taste buds exploded in delight as I sampled a berry-like liquor called Krekling. Though the Norwegian water fresh from the streams had satiated many a roadside thirst, this was better. The meal started off with a creamy fish soup, greenish in color, garnished with mussels. This too paled in comparison to the powdered soups boiled on a stove on a picnic table. Delirium nearly set in during consumption of the halibut and salmon, complemented by potatoes mixed with smoked salmon. There was spinach, carrots, mushrooms and onions topped with a white wine sauce. On top was a crayfish.

Then came dessert, a rubarb mold with chocolate and peach jam. This went down with a cloudberry liquor.

I was still in gastronomic ecstasy when we stopped at the Alta Slate Mine on the hills up out of town. Then it was over to Roger Dahl's for coffee.

Wideborg dropped me off back at the tent before saying good-night.

Exhaustion, both physical and emotional, caused me to sleep well. But early the next day, Bjøern Hansen, one of the two representatives from the Finnmark Travel Association, showed up and took me on the grand tour, stopping at Eli Jensen's house, then going on the river boat tour with Wiskøff and stuffing me with information and suggestions of various cycling routes in Finnmark.

Though it was a bit of a sensory overload, they unwittingly provided a comfort and sense of home during a time it was most needed.

They took my mind off my grandmother's death and gave me a relief from the solitude of the road.

CHAPTER FIFTEEN

Invitation To The Top Of The World

The invitation was sent through cyberspace.

"Dear Mr. Basch," it said. "We have just read about you in VG, the largest newspaper in Norway. We read that you just had left Tromsø, so we thought we had remind you to drop by Hammerfest. It might be a detour, but we guess you'll never forget the northiest (and coldest) town in the world."

The message was signed by Kaj Dahl.

Hammerfest has the distinction of being the northernmost town in the world. Though there are villages more north in Norway than Hammerfest, because of its type of government, it gets the "northernmost town in the world" label.

Hammerfest would be a bit of a detour as Dahl wrote. If North Cape is the destination, as it was, Hammerfest would be about 40 miles out of the way. That would be each way.

But that would be just fine. One doesn't turn down an offer of Norwegian hospitality.

I sent a response to Dahl's invitation and began to cycle north out of Alta on the E-6 to Hammerfest and its 9,500 residents. The road cut through the mountains, and fostered a feeling of total isolation. Clouds came down to touch the landscape. Cars had their headlights on. The temperature was dropping. Clouds and drizzle made it seem more like February than July.

It was on this road, I first saw them. First one, then two, then three.

Polar bears are scarce during the Arctic summer in Hammerfest, but the author did run into these two.

Their racks stood atop their heads. This was not a moose, so familiar in northern New Hampshire. This was not deer, another common animal. Nor was it a caribou, an animal I first saw in the far reaches of the Yukon and Alaska.

This was a trio of reindeer.

Hundreds of thousands of reindeer live near the top of the world. They live in herds and are well-suited to the cold and deep snow of the northern winters. Their broad hooves support them in the snow and their coat has a thick lower layer of curly hair which traps the air. Reindeer are the only members of the deer family where both sexes have antlers. During the year, the domestic reindeer are herded between three areas depending on the time of year. The high mountains are the summer feeding ground while mountain birch forests are sought in the autumn and spring. Pine forests are the ideal spots for winter.

Northern Finnmark, along the coast, is a network of islands connected mainly by boat. There are tunnels and bridges too. Someone told me that during the migration, the government will use large vessels to transport the reindeer from place to place when water is in the way.

Reindeer were rumored to fly, but be transported in a boat, that was a new one.

Reindeer, I was to find out, are common in this part of the world. The first sighting is always memorable. Even later that day, I was to see herds of reindeer within the Hammerfest town limits. Reindeer would follow me on roads in Sweden. They would awaken me during naps in Finland, shaking the earth as they trampled through campgrounds. I never saw one fly, but they were good eating.

They reminded me of lamb.

Though reindeer wasn't dined on that evening, pizza was. Culinary treats are regional. Take french fries for example. In certain parts of the world, they are covered in ketchup. In other parts, they are consumed with vinegar. Some have fries topped with gravy, while others can only eat them with mayonnaise.

In Hammerfest, it's Thousand Island dressing. In Scandinavia, that type of dressing is like ketchup is in the United States. Put it on fries. Put it on burgers. And if you are eating a taco pizza in the Pinocchio Pub with a pint of locally-brewed Mack beer with a couple of new-found friends, even the pizza is topped with Thousand Island dressing.

"The winter's can get boring, especially if you don't have a hobby. A lot of my friends have moved away to Oslo. They don't think there is much to do here," said Dahl.

Dahl was the guy who e-mailed me. He was sitting across the table with his girlfriend, Anita Olsen. Dahl, a 24 year-old clean cut part-time student, part-time musician who was studying to be a teacher, had been in Oslo at a Neil Young concert when he saw the newspaper article and decided to send the invitation.

That was it.

He also plays in a band. The band, called Crazy Neil and Young Horse, is obviously influenced by Young. They play cover tunes around Hammerfest and even performed a gig in a small Oslo club after the concert. Dahl and his fellow members did send an invitation to Young at his hotel to hear the band, but he didn't make it. However, Dahl did say he was told two of Young's crew members showed up.

Dahl, who has lived his whole life in Hammerfest, was with Olsen, a green-eyed teacher.

The two met me at a campground in Hammerfest and showed me around the town built among the hills near land's end. Brilliant colored houses of blue, red, pink, white and orange stood together to brighten up a land sometimes devoid of sun, where clouds sweep down and cover the mountains.

The downtown area was bustling. Buses ran through the city streets. Two statues of polar bears stood guard at the market area. Talk was of the music festival.

Kaj and Anita played tour guides. We drove up to the "Turistua" at the top of the hill "Salen." There, we had hot chocolate and coffee while overlooking the city. From customs to work, nature, cars and tourism, we all conversed trying to learn more about each other as we headed out of the city limits to a small fishing village, eventually making it back to the pub for the taco pizza.

Invited back to the apartment Kaj shared with drummer friend, Johnny, who looked like a cross between John Lennon and Frank Zappa, I spent the night. Necessities like a refrigerator, television and stereo were looked at anew by someone who had been on the road for weeks. This was the first time since the Lofoten Islands — nearly three weeks — I had slept indoors.

The four of us talked until midnight. It was about nothing in particular. Just people with common interests passing time, and gaining an enthusiasm from sharing a place called earth, but living life in different ways.

The next day I was invited to meet more of their friends who would meet at a certain time each day at a downtown restaurant "drinking coffee and waiting for the sun," someone said.

The friends came in and sat. Always coffee, always cigarettes.

This is the real reason for traveling. For just maybe two hours I got a look into the real Hammerfest, a place where people opened up and shared just a little part of their life. For two hours, I was part of their life. Maybe we could have become friends. They spoke Norwegian among themselves and switched to English while talking to me.

All of this, this small glimpse into their life, because Kaj took a chance. He read a story. He acted. I re-acted.

We said good-bye near the downtown docks. A boat would soon slice through the darkened waters of the Barents Sea, en route to Honnisvåg.

I would be on that boat, for the last leg of the journey to North Cape.

CHAPTER SIXTEEN

Seventy-One Degrees North

"I am standing here at North Cape, the extreme tip of Finnmark, literally at the end of the world. Here, where the world comes to an end, my curiosity does as well, and now I can return home content."
— *North Cape visitor Francesco Negri, 1664*

North Cape is the end of the road. For mainland Europe, you can't get any further north by road than here. It is further north than Fort Kent, Maine, more north than Whitehorse, Yukon or Yellowknife, Northwest Territories. North Cape isn't as far north as Barrow, Alaska where I once saw a resident photographed with a t-shirt that said something like: It's not the top of the world, but you can see it from here. If the weather is right, you might be able to see it from North Cape too.

North Cape is at 71 degrees north. For most people, this is as close to the top of the world as they will ever get. And every year, over 200,000 travelers make the pilgrimage to the spot, where nearly 1,000 foot cliffs plunge straight down into the cold waters of the Arctic Ocean.

On July 10, I was a sheep in the flock.

The road to North Cape was long, over 600 road miles from the Lofoten Islands. Using both road and ferries, the landscape has been dramatic fjords to thick forests to treeless tundra.

There is a campground about 16 miles from the North Cape and it is here I left most of my gear for the ride to the edge of the world. Cyclists in passing had talked about how hilly it was. Those pulling campers talked about whiteout conditions. I wanted to travel light, yet be prepared. I took one saddlebag. In it was food — bread, cold cuts and cheese. Also inside were gloves, a wool hat and waterproof shell. I wore fleece riding tights, a polypro shirt and fleece top.

Quickly, the road turned to a nine percent grade. But there was a reward — reindeer. Grunting up the hill, I saw a herd of about 30 white, gray and brown reindeer. They eyed me and didn't really think much about me until I got closer. Then, one by one, they crossed the road, their hooves clacking on the pavement. I just watched in silence, somewhat amazed.

Consuming Rudolph wasn't on my mind as I continued up. The trees disappeared and a barren landscape appeared. Soon, I entered into the fog. Visibility was near zero. As quickly as it was zero, it returned again, and the illusion was that of cycling above the clouds.

Snow, always snow, was plentiful. No, not the 10, 12 or 14 feet piled up in the winter, just a patch here and there. It's enough of a reminder of winter though.

Then, over the hills, the toll booths appear. Yes, North Cape is Norway's Mount Washington. At 6,288 feet, Mt. Washington is the highest peak in New England. Hikers can scale the mountain via several trails. The highest wind speed in the world was once recorded at its summit. A weather observatory is there and the mountain has been called "home of the world's worst weather." In winter, there is a peace and beauty above treeline. But come summer, the automobile road to the summit opens, and the procession begins. Pay the toll keeper, experience nature at her best from the safety of the car, and grab a burger and fries at the top when you are done.

There were two booths open. I got in line behind the cars, buses, motorcycles and campers. I got my credit card ready. The entrance fee was a steep $25.

"Where are you from?," asked the toll taker.

"The States," I replied.

"And you've come to see *Nordkapp*?," he asked.

"Yes," I replied.

He asked me about my trip and I told him where I had been.

He handed me back my credit card without using it.

"Sometimes we let cyclists in for free," he said.

So there I was, the last frontier, the northernmost corner of Europe. Me and a few hundred others. We went and saw the gigantic five screen video showing the area during all seasons. We saw the seven giant medals that are part of the sculpture called "Children of the Earth." We bought souvenirs. We wrote postcards. We went to the restaurant.

Reindeer graze along the hills of Norway during the summer.

The majestic cliffs, forming the last barrier against the Arctic Ocean, have for centuries been the travel destinations for both adventurers and kings. Only since 1956 have people been able to drive to North Cape. If you thumb through the brochures at North Cape, you'll learn that you can observe the midnight sun for 77 nights running, from May 12th to July 31st. That is only in theory. There was a disclaimer in the pamphlet which read, "Of course, the sun does not appear on demand, and we can just as well enjoy the sun in mid-May, on Midsummer day or at the end of July."

Snow tends to start to fall during October. But that doesn't mean that North Cape isn't visited. That's when the snow machines roar to life and mechanized-adventurers can ride their rigs to the top of the world. That's also when the midnight sun is replaced by polar nights, when the sun doesn't shine at all. During then, the northern lights dance in the sky.

This was not a place of solitude. This was more of a Disneyland, a place to move the masses in, move them out and lift a few dollars, marks, kronors or francs in the process. Solitude, or at least a better chance to find it, could have been reached via a hiking trail that was accessible from a trailhead on the road to North Cape. The six mile trail went to a point on the plateau even more north than the posh club, dining room and shops beyond the toll booths.

Instead, visitors went to the globe, marking the 71 degree spot. But in the ever-changing weather, it's not always visible. Luckily it was when I made the pilgrimage. There was a cyclist from New Zealand with his bike. He had cycled up and now stood closer to the North Pole than to Norway's largest city in the south, Oslo. He handed me his camera. I took his picture.

I handed him mine.

And there I stood, bicycle held high over the head, relishing a moment of accomplishment and thinking it can only be downhill from here, right?

CHAPTER SEVENTEEN

A Place For Those Who Don't Fit In

Sven Engholm sat at the end of his kitchen table, a cup of coffee in his hand. Near him was a poster of the Iditarod race in Alaska he had competed in just a few months before. Within view was a photo he had taken of his dog team, and a postcard signed by all the 61 racers. He was one of two Norwegians in the race that year. The other fellow countryman was Roger Dahl who I had met in Alta.

Engholm was most kind. Just a few hours earlier he had received a call from a stranger traveling by bicycle asking if he had some time for an interview.

The road to Engholm's home in the small Sami village of Karasjok also had a touch of coincidence about it. From North Cape, the road followed the sea until it headed inland, and the landscape turned from the lolling of the waves against the rocks to bush. Bush that was perfect to house restricted military areas where no stopping or photography was allowed to bush that was similar to Alaskan's interior — evergreen, low, lupine and dotted with waterways.

Like many capitals, Karasjok is located at a crossroads. It is here the Norwegian Sami parliament meets in an auditorium which houses a restaurant, shops and guest information. Prior to getting to Karasjok, I had heard about Engholm. I didn't actually know his name, but I did know that a musher of note who competed in the Iditarod lived there. Finding both his name and where he lived would be a challenge.

But it wasn't.

All I had to do was describe him at the information area. I was pointed to a flyer in English. There was his name, his address, and his phone number. When winter's snow had gone, Engholm still had a business to run and offered hiking with pack dogs during the summer. So I called. He was home. I was invited over.

Engholm, 42, is a bit of a legend in the bush of interior Finnmark. He has won its grueling 650 mile Finnmarkslopet contest an amazing 11 times since 1981. He has raced in Minnesota in the John Beargrease sled dog race, taking third in 1993 and captured the Rookie of the Year honors too. In 1994, he won the sled dog race in the Lillehammer Winter Olympics and in 1995, participated in a two-month sled dog expedition to Siberia. He has also led expeditions to Greenland and the northern reaches of Norway — Svalbard. He has received the Humanitarian Care of Dogs Award and also the Honour Award in Norway. He is also a member of the local official committee for animal rights.

But one goal had eluded him, the Iditarod.

It costs a lot of money to bring a dog team, sleds, food, equipment, family and more to Alaska from Norway. Engholm, who provides guided sled dog tours in the winter, figured he could do it for about $45,000. One thing stood in the way though — raising the money.

So in April 1995, after returning from Siberia, he received a fax that turned his dream into a path of gold.

Six years earlier, Engholm had a guest who was a very wealthy British man. The man, who Engholm wouldn't name, wanted to go into the wilderness during a one week winter sled dog tour to a place not many tourists go. Engholm brought him into places where the hopeful still pan for gold in the summer and stay in turf huts. Inside these huts are rifles, a radio, walkie-talkie's and other necessary items for wilderness life. Well, also in this hut was a sign the man found on the floor. It said: This is a place for men who don't fit in. The Englishman photographed the sign.

Engholm wasn't quite sure how the week went. The man was very quiet.

"I thought it was a bad week," said Engholm. "I was not sure if he enjoyed it."

Apparently the sign was the jewel the man had been searching for because the next year, the man returned with some friends. And the year after and the year after that. During each trip, Engholm would confide in the man, telling him how one day he would love to pilot his dog team in the race of all races.

Then came that fax. Could Engholm give him a budget to send a team to Anchorage?

Sven Engholm was one of two Norwegian competitors in the 1996 Iditarod race in Alaska.

He did.

Later on, his wife Ellen and children came over. The man did too, following Engholm's progress by plane every day. Those back home in Finnmark followed his progress on the Internet, via the race's Web site.

Engholm finished 20th in the race. On the second day, his team encountered a moose. The moose was in the middle of the trail. Engholm didn't see it, but the 16 dog team did. They stopped and started yelping.

"It was like a big ghost or monster behind some bushes," remembered Engholm.

The moose attacked. In the ensuing melee, five of the dogs were hurt.

Of those five, four were the team leaders. The lines were tangled. Engholm went for his rifle, but decided not to shoot, because soon the moose went away. The price was high. The five dogs had a mixed bag of maladies from broken legs to broken ribs. Four of the dogs had be transported by sled to the next check point seven hours away.

The dogs lived. Engholm spent $3,000 for their operations and he ended up finishing the race. The dogs were still with him the day we met, barking in the back of his home a few miles from town.

Asked about coming in 20th, Engholm just shrugs.

"The alternative was to scratch. I have much higher ambitions than that," he said.

There is a constant barking from the dogs. Just like children, they must be cared for, washed, fed and cleaned up after. Look around his kennel, his dog ranch, and see the cabins he built himself. Be invited to stay for a traditional Norwegian Saturday night dinner of porridge and meet his dog handlers. Gaze up at the bookshelf and see books written by explorers like Nansen and Amundsen. Be in the far reaches of a foreign land and be shown clippings from an Alaskan paper about a man who had been written about in your own country. You had no idea who he was until stumbling upon him in his own home.

Like his fellow mushers, Engholm talked about raising dogs and racing dogs as a lifestyle.

"Dog mushing is one of the few sports where the sexes are equal. It is one of the few sports where it is a benefit to be older, because to be good, you must know more about the sport, the training methods, nutrition, psychology, breeding and many more things," he said. "It is good if you know about all of these things."

Mushing started as hobby to the man who was born in Sweden, came to Norway in 1978 and who once made a living as a teacher educating others about the outdoors.

For Engholm, mushing started with just one dog.

"I was always interested in outdoor life. I started with one dog. He never complained. He just followed my decision. Then I started building up a sled dog team," he said.

Like the sport which now has races all over the world from South Africa to Australia to Japan to Argentina, Engholm grew too.

"The nice thing is to work as a team, to work in nature's way," he explained. "Maybe one of the best things is to realize the natural phenomenon. To just travel quiet in the winter, to see the landscape, to realize the northern lights. It is not the same in a movie, or from a house in the winter. It is a much bigger expression to be out, to be traveling in the nature."

Yes, it is good to be outside. It is good to stare nature straight in the face. Sometimes you get smacked. Sometimes you get caressed. Yes, it is good to leave the strict, organized life we humans can make for ourselves. It is good to come across people like Engholm.

Note: Sven Engholm was able to find a number of sponsors to race in the 1997 Iditarod. He finished twelfth.

CHAPTER EIGHTEEN

Fear, Doubt And Uncertainty Triumph

Fear won. Doubt triumphed. Uncertainty went home with a gold medal.

Putting it bluntly, I didn't think it would be in my best interest to go by myself with my bicycle and computer into Russia. So, I didn't.

Northern Russia has always been the "big if" in my mind during this bicycle tour. Russia has never been on my priority list of places to visit, not even on a bike. Take a look at a map though. Northern Russia and its Kola Peninsula look like a natural extension of a loop around the circle. I mean, I was so close, I had to go.

Information was hard to come by about this area in America. There was a taste from a guidebook or two, but I figured the closer I got to the border, the easier information would be to be had.

Kirkenes, Norway borders Russia. To get there, I cut right across the top of Finland from Karasjok. Kirkenes is a mining town that was Norway's most bombed village during World War II. Visitors can still go underground to the bunkers, see a film and learn about what life was like during the war.

Next door, about 100 miles away is Murmansk, the largest city in the world above the Arctic Circle. The Kola is 65,000 square miles of forest, tundra and low mountains on the Barents Sea. I learned from a guidebook I found at a hostel that it was originally populated by Sami herders and Russian trappers. When sea routes were discovered, it became a trading post. Under British pressure, Murmansk was founded in 1916. It now has over 450,000 residents.

Discovery of ore and mineral deposits accelerated growth. But that led to pollution and now the area has thousands of miles of dying forests from nickel plants.

On the map, Russia would be entered from Storskog, Norway and the road to Murmansk would pass through Nikel, Zapoljarny, Pechenga and on to the city. I would have to pedal through a strict 65 mile military zone that was only open four days a week.

While in Kirkenes, I met a handful of people familiar with the Kola. They were a virtual library of information. They told me about the pollution.

Even in the literature for travelers, there were warnings that all was not pristine on the other side of the border.

Here's what the route would entail: First would be the town of Boris Gleb, a power station where special permission was needed to visit. Then there was Nikel and its 21,000 residents. There is a nickel plant there with 6,000 employees. The facility emits "enormous amounts of sulfur dioxide. Neighbouring forests and soil are polluted by the facility," a fact sheet stated. Next was the mining town of Zapoljarny with its 23,000 people. A plant was there too. It emitted the same pollution.

I would be traveling through the Pechenga Valley, a religious, cultural and economic center of the region with its monasteries, museums and monuments. Though to the south, a huge nature preserve existed, I wasn't getting too excited about this possible leg of the journey.

From Murmansk, the road would go to Ivalo, Finland some 200 miles away with only a handful of towns along the way.

At worst though, I figured I could always go to Russia on a one-day visa-free group boat tour from Kirkenes.

And that's what I did.

I became your run-of-the-mill camera-toting, let-someone-else-do-the-driving tourist.

At 8 a.m. on July 19, the high speed catamaran began the four and a half hour excursion through the sea at the top of the world from Kirkenes. Shortly, we were in Russian waters.

Voyagers flocked to the rear of the boat when a Russian harbor pilot came aboard near Murmansk. The ship he departed from flew the Russian flag of white, blue and red. The boats were in the Kola Inlet and soon the ugliness of the waters was evident, turning the fjord into an Arctic New Jersey Turnpike. Smoke stacks bellowed foul emissions. Rotting boats, looking like submerged carcasses, lay dead in the water. The bay was filled with trawlers, cargo ships and even cruise ships. Two bright yellow

A nuclear-powered icebreaker is docked in the waters of Murmansk.

atomic ice-breakers were in port that day, used for travel near the North Pole. Even they couldn't brighten up the place.

The catamaran docked in Murmansk where we go through passport control and onto two buses. The guide welcomed us and rattles off statistics about the city, including a 15 percent unemployment rate.

"It's a mess in Russia," she says. "We don't believe anymore in communism. We want to try and be a capitalist." Try being a capitalist on the $200 to $500 a month she said Murmansk residents earn and then try to buy a three room condo for $10,000.

First stop was the Museum of Regional Studies on *prospekt* Lenina with its collection of natural history, World War II and indigenous people exhibits. Each room was guarded by an old lady whose function seemed to be opening and closing doors, turning lights on and off, and making sure no one walked off with the artifacts.

At each stop, we were surrounded by kids trying to sell pins and hats. In the 69th Parallel Hotel, we were served lunch as a six piece troupe performed Russian folk songs to tourists consuming borscht, beer, stew, coffee and pastry in a dimly lit restaurant. Here we could exchange our money for rubles (5,000 to the dollar) and warned we couldn't take rubles out of the country, so change your money accordingly.

Just two weeks after a nation had embraced democracy and rejected communism once again, the tour guide was pointing out the sights in the city.

The bus was making its way down the main street when she called attention to a restaurant called Burger Bar. Even at $7 a burger, it was popular with the young and trendy in Murmansk. Plus, another big clientele was the Mafia.

She acknowledged there was a battle going on in this northern Russian city as different groups fight for their turf. "But don't worry," she said, "they are only after rich businessmen and not common people."

Around the city we went, passing decaying city buses, buildings that needed one, two and three coats of paint, the old offices of the KGB and unkempt trees placed haphazardly between road and sidewalks. There was the statue of Anatoly Bredov, a Russian hero who surrounded by Germans during World War II, coaxed a few of the Nazis closer before detonating a grenade. He is shown moments before impact. Along the way we were shown central square, *Pyat-Ugla* or Five Corners. Here we took an hour to explore the largest department store in Murmansk, Volna. In its three stories, there were television sets, tents, meat, boxes of orange juice, suits, dresses, fur hats, posters of Michael Jackson, video games, Pat Boone albums, vodka and more. There were no aisles to shop through, just a long dark hall with items stocked behind barriers with attendants. Perhaps most remarkable was that purchases were totaled with an abacus.

Next we were whisked to the 450 foot high "Alyosha," a monument to the soldiers of World War II, towering above the city near Lake Semyonovskaya. Though newly engaged couples traditionally come to "Alyosha" to drink a good-luck bottle of champagne, there wasn't anything terribly romantic about the view.

Then it was off to St. Nicholas Church, located in a rundown section of the city with crumbling wooden homes. The church was pewless, as the faithful pray on their knees.

The tour ended back at the docks where we said good-bye to our guides and Murmansk. Once on the boat, we soon returned the Russian pilot to his craft. Then, an announcement came that a Russian submarine was in the waters near us. We flocked outside to see it and then the flurry of picture taking began.

The whirls of the shutters sounded across the sea as we captured yet another glimpse of Russia before heading back into the nuclear-free waters of Norway.

Ugliness is a part of travel. It should be experienced so one can see what neglect and irresponsibility can do.

I decided not to return to Russia, even now armed with a map of Murmansk, knowing where the hotels were and an idea that I would be able to decipher some of the Cyrillic alphabet. The decision was the right one for me. However, what gnawed at me was the lesson learned. I reached a limit I never knew I had. An intangible fear became real.

I came to know fear that day.

It's strange the fear we carry inside, sometimes not even knowing that we have it. Just two days before my tourist trip to Russia, a commercial airliner, TWA Flight 800, exploded thousands of miles away in America. Everyone on board was killed as the flight went down in Long Island Sound. That's Long Island, New York, the place where I grew up. Even months after the accident, there was no official explanation for the crash. Was it a terrorist? Was it a missile? Was it mechanical failure?

Then, some ten days later, a bomb in a knapsack exploded in Atlanta, Georgia during the summer Olympic games. The Olympics, a symbol of international unity, was being played out in the home of the free and the brave. Who planted the bomb? Was it a terrorist? Was it an American? Months later, there still wasn't an explanation.

There I was, snubbing Russia. Had I been a foreigner considering a trip to America, would I go knowing that airliners blow up and people detonate bombs during games of brotherhood?

With a newfound fear tucked deep inside me, I got on my bicycle and headed to the lakes, woods and taiga of Finland.

CHAPTER NINETEEN

Great Mosquito Wars

The Finns have got to be the friendliest people in the world. That was my first thought, leaving the majestic country of Norway, and heading into Finland via the Tana River valley on July 22. They always seemed to be waving. But they weren't saying hello.

It was the mosquitoes.

Big, fat, aggressive, human-chomping mosquitoes live in the Arctic. They are so huge, radio stations and newspapers in the region have had contests where listeners and readers send in the biggest, dead mosquito they've killed. Along the coast, they are tolerable. Now inland, among the evergreens, lakes, hills and rivers, they were pests.

Mosquitoes were everywhere. There were oils, lotions, ointments, sprays, coils and nets to combat the Finnish Air Force. What was amazing, was that there were actually people in short-sleeved shirts fly-fishing (Finns love to fish) who were seemingly immune from the evil creatures.

Finns, along with having some of the longest names for places I've ever seen, had a passion for wearing fatigues. At least the males did. This seemed to be standard outdoor wear, along with knife in a sheath, and perhaps a wooden cup hanging from the belt loop.

Maybe this was a way to fight the insects.

Immunity, or constant smoldering fires, looked to be the chief ways to do battle with the bugs. To be fair, the Great Mosquito Wars actually began for me in inland Norway, in Karasjok. It was there, the mosquitoes and I began the first of many battles.

The tent was often the battleground. Though they are hard to see, mosquitoes have rather large noses I think. This is how they smell human blood, which to them, is a meal. Thus, all cyclists become some sort of a meal on wheels for the airborne patrol. The soldiers wait for the meal to dismount and set up a tent.

Once the targeted meal is inside, the assembled wait. Their preferred waiting room is just outside the tent's screen. Often, their shadows could be seen from inside the tent. They would frequent the area between the tent's fly and the actual structure itself. They would land on the tent. They would buzz.

They would then wait for the target to leave the tent, and pounce on said target. Target would wave hands incessantly. Target would slap own arms, ankles, neck, wrists, forehead, thighs, shoulders. There would be casualties. But the soldiers would persist.

They were tenacious fighters. The mosquitoes would find every unexposed patch of flesh. A padded bicycle glove would cover most of the hand. They would attack the exposed fingers and circle of flesh on the hand. A successful sweep behind the ears probably resulted in some Badge of Honor from a battalion commander. They could pierce polypro socks, polypro tops, and fleece. Though insect repellent was applied, they would find that one minute section of flesh in some foreign fold of the body that had been missed. They would send communications to their comrades. They would attack, sting and conquer.

As the target was exiting the tent, troops would mount assaults on several fronts. While the target was madly waving its arms, trying to fasten the zipper to close the tent, suicide bombers would enter the tent.

There, they would wait until the target returned and launch a night attack.

The internal tent battles were bloody affairs. In war, opponents learn each others' ways. After the target becomes a bicycling Braille billboard with red pock-marked scars on ankles, wrists and fingers, it starts thinking about a pre-emptive strike.

The suicide bombers and the battalions situated on the outside of the tent were prime prey.

In the evening, during the season of the midnight sun, the mosquitoes would assemble for a dawn respite from the day's assaults. They would perch themselves on the tent. Since there was light, they would be visible in the form of shadows. The shadows were easy pickings for a finger zinger.

The finger zinger is an old technique of doing battle with the mosquito. It is very easy to learn. The index finger of either hand is curled in an arc with the nail flush against the meaty front of the thumb. The target, either flat on its back or from a kneeling position, selects a shadow and slowly extends the cocked weapon towards the enemy. The enemy, now regaling its comrades with tales of the day, is momentarily caught off guard.

When the cocked weapon is within striking range, the index finger is released, smacking the tent with a ping, and sends the enemy crashing into the fly. The enemy is either knocked out, killed, or comes back for more.

The finger zinger, along with the traditional squash or slap technique, was employed during the suicide bomber attacks in the middle of the night. The beauty of the silent Arctic night would often be tainted by the buzz of the bugs. The suicide bombers would wait until the target tried to fall asleep. Their constant drone would keep said target awake. The buzz around the head after a long day of cycling can be irritating.

There were times when the target could actually reach out and catch the mosquito in mid-flight, then crush it. The carcass would then fall to the ground and wait for the morning removal.

The target could also chase squadrons around the tent, slapping and squashing them against the tent walls. This would result in blood-stained splotches around the tent.

In the morning, the carcasses would be removed, by sweeping them by hand out of the tent.

The Great Mosquito Wars were not limited to the tent. They were also fought during the day, often by the side of the road, when the target would stop and rest.

The target was not without protection. Repellent was applied on a daily basis. Another protective device the target could use was a net.

The mosquito net is a silly looking contraption, especially viewed from the eyes of a target who hails from a part of the world where the nets aren't used by many people. The mosquito net was something to be pointed to in an equipment catalog and cackled at with comments like, "Do people actually use those things?"

They do.

There are different types of nets to choose from. One could say there are several styles, and one could make quite a fashion statement.

The American target was carrying a net that was a bit Frankenstein-esque. There was a squareness about it that made it unattractive. A pair of cords hung down from the base of the net. These cords would be tied under each armpit. This was how the net stayed in place.

There were other types too. Others were square, but had an elastic cord at the base. Some appeared to be circular and had a tighter fit on the wearer. And some appeared to be attached to a hat. How chic! Please do not have visions of a cyclist wearing a mosquito net while riding. This did not happen.

What did happen was that the net had to be used during rest stops, particularly while eating. Trying to eat, while wearing a mosquito net is not something everyone must do. Should you do it, stay away from items such as peanut butter and jelly. Though fine for trapping the renegades, there are better ways to ingest protein. The mosquitoes, in their feeding frenzy, can get stuck in the spread and make it down the ol' gullet. Realization of such an act results in a coughing spree, which again, while wearing a mosquito net, can be quite messy.

The act of eating becomes a race as one hand must hold the food, while the other lifts the base of the net above the mouth. The food is placed in the mouth rather quickly and then the hand that lifts the net then releases it. As the process continues, the cords which are tied under the armpit are stretched. This loosens them and can result in a picayune gap that only a skilled flying militiaman can negotiate. The unwanted intruder is, literally, in the target's face. This puts a damper on the meal. The intruder buzzes about, and its' buzz is often quite loud to the ear. One way to eliminate the pest is to catch it in the folds of the net. The dead insect then falls to the little dimple-like cavity in the base of the neck where it is removed.

Of course, all these Great Mosquito Wars could have been avoided by applying yet another insect-avoidance technique — staying indoors. The Finns would also fight the mosquitoes at their door fronts. Long plastic strips would hang from the doors to keep the mosquitoes out. This apparently worked.

But remaining indoors was an option never considered.

CHAPTER TWENTY

Road Warriors

They were at a roadside rest area outside the Sami town of Utsjoki. The little girl was at a picnic table, drawing with colored pencils, while the other blonde, her mother, was smoking a cigarette and reading a book. The girl was wearing a mosquito net. The mother had the cigarette, which seemed to be her defense against the swarm. Their bicycles and gear were leaning against the outhouse.

They too, were taking a break from the Arctic heat during their journey from Hamburg, Germany.

The mother spoke English. The little girl didn't. How strange it must be for a child to hear a parent chatting away and not being able to understand a word. How wonderful it must be at the same time to be introduced to a new language, hearing it straight from the mouth of your mom.

The mother, was a former architect, now out of work, with a three year-old daughter staying back home with her mother. She wasn't married. She said she was trying to change her life, and the bicycle was a vehicle for that change.

Change is a constant theme in the bicycle touring world. It knows no boundaries. It knows no language. It knows no color. Change is universal. And here it was coming again, this time with a touch of a German accent. It came with an Icelandic spice when spoken by Björgvin Holm in his tent while in Akranes. It had come with accents all across roads traveled in the United States and Canada.

Whatever became of the mother and daughter cycling duo from Germany?

Those seeking a break from the mundane aspects of life took to the road. If they had lost a job, they rode. Celebrating a 50th birthday or the like? Been divorced? Hop on that bike. Just been through some major surgery or battle with a killer in the form of a disease? See ya. It's road trip time.

It comes down to the challenge, the exploration. The world spins a bit more slowly from the seat of a bicycle. Without the media assault through the newspapers, television or radio, thought turns to purity again. Though the rider could be blissfully unaware of global events, thoughts turn inside. The rider can think again. The rider can tap forgotten and dormant reservoirs of the mind and soul. It is a time for self-discovery, or re-discovery. It's a time to rely on yourself; a time to remember the things you can do, and can't do. It's a time to burst out loud with laughter from a memory. It's a time to sing. It's a time to nap. It's a time to eat when you're hungry and not because the clock strikes noon.

It's a time to re-adjust, re-acquaint and re-energize.

Perhaps this is what the mother was doing. Perhaps it's what every traveler is doing.

The mother had decided to return to a sport she knew as a teen-ager. This wasn't the first trip the mother and daughter were on. A year earlier the two had taken a shorter trip, and done some riding in Denmark and Germany.

Now, in five weeks, the two had covered 1,000 miles, riding from Helsinki, Finland to Kirkenes, Norway and were now heading back.

There were a number of incredible aspects about their adventure. First was that a mother and daughter could actually travel together, camp together and eat together for 1,000 miles and one hadn't killed the other.

Secondly, the bikes they were riding were ancient. The mother was on a 10-speed bike that was between 15 and 20 years old. It had a broken brake and not all the gears worked. She was having trouble with the rim and spokes and had to walk on a lot of the hills.

The girl, who could not have been more than 12, was even more incredible. She was on a little three-speed bike. Her gear-shifting choices were simple — this one, that one and the other one.

The mosquitoes loved the little girl. When she took off the net, red splotches could been seen on her face.

She wore blue jeans and a long sleeved shirt. There was no helmet. No bicycling shoes with clips. No padded shorts. No bicycling gloves.

The mother had similar riding attire. Probably in her mid-30's, she wore long pants, long sleeved shirt and a scarf around her neck. They carried a tent, sleeping bags and saddlebags on the back of their bicycles. The bicycles had fenders on them. That seemed to be standard fare for touring Europeans. Americans apparently can't be bothered. It's added weight, you know.

They roughed it too. Campgrounds weren't slept in every night. They too would take advantage of the "Everyman's right" and just pitch a tent in the woods. They rode between 40 and 50 miles per day.

How I wished I could talk to that little girl. I wished the mother spoke better English so we could take the conversation a little deeper.

We rode together for awhile, both heading in the same direction, south. Like she said she did, the mother would stop and walk up some of the hills. The little girl didn't say much. She would just stand up on the pedals and grunt.

What was this girl thinking? What sort of woman would she grow up to be? What kind of mother could leave one daughter home and take one daughter on the road?

These questions went unanswered. We rode together for a few miles, but their pace was slow. I crested a hill and they were gone.

We did meet up again that night at a campground in the junction town of Kaamanen.

"My daughter said, and now we will meet the American," she said in the campground kitchen, preparing a meal of pancakes, pasta, tomato sauce and onions. The cigarette smoke rose in the air during her four cups of coffee.

The mother and daughter became some of the nameless figures you meet on the road. They appear in your life for a few miles, and then they are gone, except for the memories they leave behind.

Though the mother was given an address and a request for a postcard upon completion of their journey, one never came.

Though not as steep as the fjords and mountains of Iceland and Norway, the Finnish hills, combined with the heat, made the bicycle tired. Every once in awhile, it would tell me to get off the saddle and take it for a walk. I would comply.

Outside the ski town of Saariselka, the bike asked to be walked.

There I was, taking it on a walk, when another two-wheeled adventurer slowed down. He gave me the thumbs up sign. He was checking to see if all was well with the bike and I.

I indicated all was well with my very own thumbs up sign.

Nonetheless, the man on the motorcycle pulled over, cut his engine and took off his helmet.

"Everything okay?," he asked.

I explained it was. Sometimes I just like to walk.

"I could pull you," he said.

That would be a new one. But I passed on the idea.

"Are you that guy bicycling around the Arctic Circle?," he asked.

"Yeah," was the answer.

"I've heard about you," he said.

This was Neale Bayly, a 34 year-old Brit living in Florida where he worked as a motorcycle mechanic. The day before, he had met the nameless mother and daughter cycling team. He had given the girl some candy and said she wasn't feeling too well. That's how he heard about the cycling American with a laptop.

Bayly was a bit of a motorized adventurer. He was riding his bike affectionately named Laura.

In 1986, he and his ex-wife had ridden a 13 year-old motorcycle which cost $400, 10,000 miles from Florida to Alaska. They carried a small tent and bought their clothes along the way from the Salvation Army. They abandoned the rig in Tok, Alaska and then hitchhiked to Redding, California from there. He said it was a 3,400 mile ride with one trucker that lasted seven days. Bayly thought that ride could have been some sort of hitch-hiking record.

He had done some backpacking in Southeast Asia and Australia, plus ridden his motorcycle all over Europe. One year he rode 10,000 miles through Australia. In 1995, he rode 5,000 miles with friends from Guatemala to Peru.

When we met, he was five weeks into a ride of northern Europe, and was thinking of heading to Istanbul, Turkey and Spain.

Clearly, this was a man who loved motorcycles. But an industrial accident in 1988 left him with back problems. Over the years, he gained a new spine. In his spine was a four-inch bolt, a piece of someone else's leg bone, a piece of his hip bone and a screw with washers. He even showed me the scar right there by the side of the road.

What took a few moments to realize, was that we were both overjoyed at being able to speak English at our normal pace. Granted, his had a British accent, and mine was American-flavored, but we were able to ramble right along. He had just spent a few days riding with a Belgian couple and was starting to tire of grade school textbook English. I felt his pain.

We just swapped traveling stories by the roadside for what had to be about a half hour. One story floored me. Not because it was outrageous. After all, a man riding a motorcycle with someone else's body parts in his back is fairly outrageous. Instead, it was the last of three "small world" stories I had accumulated over the miles.

I have always been amazed at the smallness of the world during travel. You are always bound to meet someone who knows someone who knows you or someone who has been to a place near where you live. I've had some amazing tales myself during other adventures, but I wasn't expecting much on a trip to northern Europe.

The first touch of a "small world-itis" was in Iceland when I had been befriended by the search and rescue team who took me on the glacial hike and into the ice cave. They had all sorts of climbing equipment. The harnesses they were wearing had been manufactured by a company called Wild Country, which has an outfit a few miles from my house.

Then there was Norway. I'm cycling outside of Kirkenes near the Russian border. A blaze of color passes me on roller skis. We exchange pleasantries. I continued cycling and make it to a roadside pull-off and examine a map. The blaze returns and stops. We chat.

His name is Krister Sørgård. Yeah, he's training. That's because he is a member of the Norwegian national ski team.

Cool, I say. We talk some more. He's getting married in a few days, he says. Cool, I say. I talk some more. I tell him I reside in a place where two members of the US Olympic Ski Team who competed in the 1994 Olympics in Lillehammer live. Maybe he knew Marcus Nash or Carl

Swenson?

He knew Swenson. That past winter, he shared a bus with him a few times during the World Cup race circuit.

Then there was this hill in Finland and the meeting with Bayly. He tells me about a book he liked about a guy who rode his motorcycle all over the world. It's called "Jupiter's Travels" and about this rider who passed through 54 countries in four years on a motorcycle. Bayly told me he had purchased the book from an outfit called Whitehorse Press. Whitehorse Press is a business in the Mount Washington Valley of New Hampshire, where I live.

Bayly and I finished our roadside stop and swap. We both continued down the same road, yet each having different adventures.

Note: There is a postscript to the Bayly story. We kept in touch, and he informed me he tallied 17,500 miles during that summer and visited the most northern, eastern, western and southern points of Europe. He wanted to know if I got his postcard. I told him I didn't. A shame, he said. He had given the postcard to a girl he had traveled with for a few days. "She said she met you at the hostel in Stamsund, Norway," Bayly said.

Is that a small world or what?

CHAPTER TWENTY-ONE

A Whole Lot Of Shaking Going On

In a crowd of characters, the foreigner stood out. It's best that he not be identified by name because of what he wore. No, it wasn't the Australian flag — blue, red and white — standing high in his hat, with pins and a pair of koala bears. That's not why he won't be identified. Then you look closer and your jaw drops. Around his neck and blurring his lucky number 13 entry are three, count 'em three, gold nuggets.

"Don't tell anyone," he says. "But I'm traveling with over $80,000 worth of gold with me." The Aussie struck gold in the summer of 1995 in Coloma, California, finishing third in the U.S. National Goldpanning Championships.

Gold was everywhere the first weekend in August in the tiny Arctic village of Tankaavara in northern Finland as over 300 competitors, mainly from Finland, vied for the title in the Finland Goldpanning Open. Sweden, Germany, Denmark and Australia were represented too in this beer-for-breakfast, pass-the-vodka-bottle, let's-sing-another-song, nugget of an event.

Travel in northern climes by bicycle and gold is bound to find you. James Wilson Marshall found gold in a Sierra Nevada mountains' sawmill on January 24, 1848 and triggered the California Gold Rush. Alaska was the site of a gold rush in 1898 while the Yukon experienced gold fever two years earlier. Finland is no different. The country has produced alluvial gold for the last 400 years and during this time, history has re-

The Finnish Goldpanning Championships attracted competitors of all ages.

corded stories of personal fortunes, tragic bankruptcies, successful gold rushes as well as hard times, according to a history ledger.

Northern Finland, or Lapland, had its run for the nugget in 1868. The Ivalo Gold Rush attracted 500 miners.

Now, gold panning is a hobby. A few can make a living at it. Mostly though, it's a golden hue for the tourism industry where vacationers can walk through a re-created boom town and pan for their own gold.

But these 300 or so enthusiasts had real gold on their mind. The top male and female finishers here got free trips to the World Goldpanning Championships in Dawson Creek, Yukon that summer.

The gist of the games are simple: find the golden chips hidden in the sand in the least amount of time and you win the trophy.

The stands were filled with enthusiasts on the cool, rainy weekend. Hats were fashionable. Wide-brimmed hats held pins, swatches of cloth, feathers and animal skins. Beards were fashionable too. At least, they were for the men.

Imagine taking a gold pan and having to wash through a few pounds of sand to find maybe eight or nine flecks of gold while a crowd of gold watchers cheer you on. That's what the competition was like.

No more than 30 panners of both sexes and ages competed at a time. Of course, you could bring your own pan, and it must comply with certain depth and width regulations.

The competitors would cross over a bridge to a field of 30 small washing pools. First, they were all given buckets of sand. Earlier, these buckets were seeded with minute flakes of gold. Each bucket had the same amount of pieces (the number not announced) and weighed the same. Then, you are given a test tube. You fill the tube half way with water. Gold will be put into the tube. With the water, it's easier to see the gold, or *kulta* in Finnish.

Armed with pan, sand and tube, you make your way to your pool. Maybe you splash around in your knee-high boots to level the ground. Perhaps you douse your pan. The tube is put in a holder.

The tension mounts. The introductions are made. The competitors face the announcer and await the signal. There it is and the rush begins.

Competitors grab the buckets of sand, hurriedly pouring the contents into the pan and then flinging the buckets with a clang on to the ground. Some sit, others stand and the water becomes a gold shark feeding frenzy. They shake, shift, swirl and sift the golden sands, throwing away stones and breaking down the clay. Round and round they swish through the water, depleting the sand. One and two minutes go by.

As the faster panners start to finish up, watch closely. They skillfully reach for the test tube and with an index finger, pick up the flecks and insert them into the tube. Like a surgeon, they then put the cap on the tube. In a burst of action, they raise the pan over their heads to announce they are finished. The tubes are brought to a judge who counts the specks.

If you didn't find them all, five minutes is added to your time for each one not in the tube.

At the end of two days, the winners are named, and those at the top of the divisions are awarded medals and no doubt go home with golden dreams in their heads.

CHAPTER TWENTY-TWO

What Would Rudolph Say?

The Great Bearded One was having a problem. There was a family, complete with mom, dad, grandma, grandpa and a couple of kids who were jabbering on about something.

One might think Old Jolly One could understand everything. After all, he's the great omnipotent one. He is everywhere and sees everything. Santa knows if you've been bad or good, so be good for goodness sake.

Though Santa is probably King of the Frequent Flyer miles, he still couldn't make sense of that gibberish, which was just a language he didn't know.

So what's Santa to do?

"I don't understand," he said in English with a touch of a Finnish accent.

He threw in a few words of Spanish. Maybe that was Portuguese they were babbling. That didn't work.

No matter. The gnomes in the workshop snapped the photo. The high-tech helper than scanned the picture into the computer and in a few minutes, the photo was theirs for about ten bucks.

Welcome to Santa's Village on the Arctic Circle.

It's so tacky you've just got to love it. The village is located on the Arctic Circle, some six mile north of the city of Rovaniemi. There are even signs indicating where the Arctic Circle begins. It's right across from the gas station. Basically, Santa's workshop is a mall with goods to buy, a

114

post office for sending little Jimmy and Suzie a Christmas card straight from the Number One Guy himself and a cafe. Of course, Santa's an expanding man. So in the summer of 1996, they were building him a new office and restaurant. Hey, it's a long, tough journey to the Arctic. You've got to eat. You've got to rest.

Santa's reindeer were there too. There was a puppet theater, an observation tower, polar museum, and an outdoor Arctic sport exhibit. The Finns were in the running for the kitsch of the year award.

Santa was a bit thinner than I had imagined. I guess the summer does that to a man. He was probably out riding his bike or running since there isn't any snow on the ground. Then again, maybe summer is just a lean time for the King of Winter. He did have his white beard and red jacket. He wore black pants and brown boots as he sat in his regal chair, holding forth in his Finland kingdom. The area around his throne looked like a child's room. There was a bed, stuffed toys, a Christmas tree and a small fireplace in the corner.

During a lull in the procession, I asked him a couple of questions, like which languages he spoke.

"I speak all languages because I have been all over the world," said the man the Finns call Joulupukki. I called him Santa though. Can't say Joulupukki.

I didn't want to confront the guy over that exchange just a few minutes before. There are a few things I wanted under my tree during the upcoming holiday season and it didn't make sense to jeopardize their delivery.

"So, Santa," I said. "Where do your visitors come from?"

"They come from Italy, France, China, Japan, all over," said the thin man. "All over. Mostly we speak English. There are so many different languages."

There were a couple of families starting to line up. Time was short. So I fired away one more question.

"How do you know who's been good?"

"I have my small helpers," said Joulupukki. "They are looking and watching all over the world. They look into houses and know everything."

This was startling. I wanted to ask him if Peeping Tom was a little helper then, but I couldn't stand in the way of the people behind me.

Kids came up to him. He switched from English to German in a reindeer hoof beat. Some kids didn't know what to make of the guy. They were timid. Others weren't at all, rattling off a list that Santa would check twice.

The tourists took their own photos, ignoring the posted signs in Russian, English, German, Norwegian and Finnish requesting flashes not be used. Santa was good about it. He didn't say anything. Nor did the little helpers.

If you didn't want to shell out your finnmarks or francs or whatever currency you were carrying for photos, that wasn't a problem. They would tag your wallet another way. Mail a letter from Santa to a loved one at Christmas for a few bucks.

Yes, they marketed Santa just right. He has his own home page and you could even e-mail the man. There was even a station with several computers with Santa CD's that told the story of how Santa chose Finnish Lapland over Norway, Sweden, the North Pole and Greenland as his home. All places claim to be home to Father Christmas.

His Finland home is located at 66 degrees, 33 minutes north, just barely above the Arctic Circle. The Swedes call him Jultomte and say he hails from Mora. The Norwegians call him Julnisse and say he lives near Oslo, in the town of Droback. The Danes call him Juleman and say he comes from Greenland. Americans call him Santa Claus and say he comes from the North Pole. I have visited North Pole, Alaska, outside of Fairbanks. Didn't bump into Santa at the fast food restaurant I visited passing through.

The Finns make a good point though as to why Santa comes from Lapland.

"We could point out important fact," I read. "Only Finnish Lapland is the natural home for reindeer. This is why Santa Claus has chosen to settle in Finnish Lapland which is home to around 300,000 reindeer and only 200,000 people."

That's a good point. But I wanted to learn more about the Santa man. I came across the following story (complete in strange English), provided by his little helpers in a three-page handout to visiting journalists on bicycles:

"It is a well-known fact, that when bringing the presents to the people all over the world at Christmas, Santa Claus is traveling with his reindeers. The reindeers, and especially Santa's reindeers, led by Rudolph, are living in Lapland. This was partially, the reason why Santa Claus chose to settle down to live in the Finnish Lapland.

Santa Claus, or Father Christmas as he is also called in English, has his house in the quiet wilderness, among the fells of the eastern part of Lapland. His home fell is called Korvatunturi, which in English, means "Earfell." The name comes from the fact, that the fell looks like two animal ears sticking up and listening to something. It is said that this is how Santa Claus can hear all the children in the world.

Santa Claus' home, however, is a very secret place, and he cannot invite any visitors there. He wishes to have his quiet moments there, to rest after busy seasons, and then he has all his Christmas secrets there, and naturally they cannot be shown to anybody before Christmas time. So it is because of this, that Santa Claus has a house at the Arctic Circle, near the city of Rovaniemi. The building of this place started in 1950, when the first cottage there was built.

The house of Santa Claus is made of round logs. The house inside is decorated both with Christmas decorations and some old pieces he has collected and kept through the centuries. At this house you can meet him practically every day of the year. And he does have a lot of visitors, the estimate is about a half a million annually. Opposite his house is his post office, where the hundreds of thousands of letters from all over the world arrive. Last year he received letters from about 150 countries. He tries, with his helpers, to answer all the letters.

Santa Claus travels also quite a lot outside the Christmas season. He makes goodwill visits to different countries and visits children's hospitals, schools, kindergartens, etc. Through his travels, his wide correspondence and the many visitors he has, Santa Claus follows widely what is happening in the world. He is quite worried about some of the things which are happening. He is especially concerned about the welfare of children. He cares about nature, because he lives within it himself and realizes just how important it is to mankind. Even though Santa Claus is always happy to meet people, he also enjoys quiet moments in the wilderness and fells surrounding him and spends a lot of time listening to nature.

How old is Santa Claus? Well, how old is a dream? When asked this question, he tells how he was sitting one evening in his rocking chair and was trying to remember how many Christmases he could remember. When he was coming to somewhere near 350, he fell asleep.

Has he got children? Yes, all the children of the world are his children and he loves them all.

How many elves has he got? There must be several hundreds of them, but as they are always running around, he can never really count them. But remember, you can also be Santa Claus' helper. When you bring happiness and joy to someone, you really are Santa's helper.

How many reindeer has he got? Only the wind that blows over the fells knows exactly, but there are more than there are rivers in the wilderness, but less than there are snowflakes on a December night."

Wow! This Santa sounded like a great guy. But this reindeer thing had me a little concerned. As I was walking around the village, I wondered how Rudolph and his seven other sleigh-pulling compatriots felt. Sure, there were places for the kids to play. There were shops with all sorts of goods like t-shirts, knives, candles and jewelry. But there were also souvenirs like reindeer leather, antlers and foods. Reindeer skins were commonplace. In one shop, the shelves were filled with cans of reindeer soup and stew. There were even reindeer balls. These were made of licorice. Rudolph may not have been the only creature not sleeping well near the Arctic Circle. Yogi the Bear might have been tossing and turning. There was bear soup. And Charlie the Tuna, well, he might not have run at the mouth had he seen the trout soup for sale.

At least there wasn't any Prancer pastrami or Rudolph ratatouille on the shelves. Well, at least none that I saw.

CHAPTER TWENTY-THREE

The Ultimate Paddling Test

Jamie Christie was munching a well-deserved apple. The 24 year-old British kayaker, ranked 37th in the world, had just finished paddling about 60 miles down the Tornio River on the hottest day of summer with the mercury hovering near 90 degrees.

It had been a tough day for him. Christie, and others who paddle the World Cup circuit, are accustomed to courses that are maybe three or four miles, and are completed in 20 to 25 minutes.

Christie and about 65 competitors from six countries were on day four of what many considered to be the ultimate test for a paddler — the Arctic Canoe Race, a 350 mile challenge along a river that straddles Finland and Sweden.

"There's no other race in the world like this. It's just a famous race. I had to come here. It's far away from everything, in the middle of nowhere. It's just something you have to do," he said.

From Russia to South Africa, they have been coming to nowhere since 1983 to battle the Arctic wilderness for seven days. Starting from the source of the river near the Norwegian border in Kilpisjarvi, they paddle until it empties into the Gulf of Bothnia. Two-thirds of the race is above the Arctic Circle. Competitors can fight snow, rain, hail, cold, mosquitoes and the heat on any given day. They have to navigate through 140 rapids. They must also make their way through long stretches of flat water.

Sounds crazy, huh? Yet year after year, they keep coming back. The

There is sun in the Arctic Circle. This paddler is covered with sunscreen as she prepares to take to the water in the Arctic Canoe Race.

pros compete for glory and a few bucks, while others actually come to have fun and take part in the rally section of the journey, taking in the scenery along Europe's longest free-flowing river.

That's what I was doing when I stumbled across the race. Actually, I was sleeping at a campground in Kolari, Finland on the Swedish border. The heat, during the actual ten days of summer they have near the top of the world, called for a nap. When I laid down, I was the only tent in the campground.

When I woke up, there was the Arctic Canoe Race.

Seriously.

Race headquarters came right up to the tent in the form of a long converted bus which acted as the mobile race center. Then came the drivers. Then came the boats. Then came the stories, and a meeting with a Finnish reporter from a local paper. He also did the media coverage for the event and spoke excellent English.

The next thing you know, I'm hooking up the laptop to an outlet outside and the interviews began.

Riita Nicholson, who lives outside of Helsinki, Finland's largest city, has been navigating the Arctic waters three times. Before that, she volunteered for five races as a support crew member. She takes part in the rally and now looks at the race as a vacation and a way to see friends.

Some of the rapids are Finland's fiercest. Knowing a rescue team is nearby makes negotiating them easier. While paddling, she's seen reindeer and salmon. Of course, she's also experienced the ever-changing weather.

"Quite often it can be cold, but you get used to it. It can be cold and rainy, but this is a water sport. It doesn't matter where the water comes from. You get used to it. With the proper gear, you don't get cold," she said.

For the racers, the ACR is a marathon unlike no other. The race is similar to the Tour de France bicycle race with various stages from sprints to marathons to mass starts. The winner receives no points. The person with the least amount of points at the end of the race is the winner.

Each racer has a story. There's Vaino Palotiita of Finland. At 60, he's competed in every Arctic Canoe Race. Then there is Heiz Rodinger of Austria. He's 55 and has been in the race six times. Rodinger is Europe's Ironman on water. A member of the 1972 Austrian Olympic team, he is in the German edition of the Guiness Book of World Records for the most kilometers ever paddled. He entered the book at 162,000 (about 100,000 miles) and now has accumulated 176,000.

"I'm 55 and always want to know how good I am. I always want to know if I can still do this. This is a test," he said before getting into his kayak. "The first time is the last time for the young people. They don't come again. Once and that is it."

This is not only a test on water, but a test on the wallet and in logistics. Northern Finland is up there and for anyone coming from England or Germany, it can take a while to get up there. Entrants can bring two boats. They bring food, gear, car, and support staff. They don't fly here. They drive. For Rodinger and crew, it was 35 hours. Then the crew drives the gear from start to finish each day. Often, paddlers spend from 7 to 14 hours a day on the water, traveling distances from 37 to 65 miles per day.

At night, they are tired. But never tired enough to quaff down a few beers after the long paddle.

And then at night, there is another obstacle — the sun. In August, the sun is just beginning to dip below the horizon. At 10 p.m., you can still read a newspaper in your tent.

"Sleeping is a problem," said Christie. "There is light coming in the tent all the time."

But it didn't bother Christie that summer. He won the race.

CHAPTER TWENTY-FOUR

Sheriff Of The Midnight Sun

The king and queen of Sweden were wed in 1976, but it wasn't until 15 years later that a special present reached them and because of that present, the "midnight sun sheriff of Pajala" was born.

A knife had been hand-crafted by a Sami resident of northern Sweden. About 30 centimeters in length, the craftsman spent long hours, meticulously putting together the royal gift. The skilled artisan could not make the long journey down to the south of Sweden to present the gift to the newlyweds. Instead, he gave the knife to his son and told him to go to Stockholm and give it to his king and queen.

The son took the knife, but the gift never made it to the couple. The son gave the knife to a friend. For a decade, the whereabouts of the knife were unknown. But one day, the knife-maker learned that the gift was in America, in Boston. The knife was retrieved.

He wanted to give his son a second chance.

So he gave him the same knife and told him to go to Stockholm and give it to the king and queen.

The son took the knife.

The knife didn't make it to Stockholm — again.

The knife disappeared again for a few years, but didn't cross the sea to America this time.

There are six policemen in Pajala. They serve and protect the 8,000 people in this northern county where the last murder took place some 20 years ago. People don't lock their homes.

One of the policeman, Åke Siikavaara, heard about the knife. He and a friend were able to track it down to a knife collector's home in Pajala in 1991 and decided to make the collector an offer. They bought the knife. This time they didn't entrust the son to carry the knife to the king and queen. They decided to do it themselves.

Siikavaara is known in these parts as being somewhat of a showman. Adventurer, hunter, horseman and law enforcer, he and the friend made the decision to deliver the knife to the royal couple themselves. So in 1991, they took a trailer and two reindeer and made a one-week journey of about 700 miles to the palace in Stockholm.

And there, albeit 15 years late, they presented the king and queen with their wedding gift.

The journey was heralded by the media from many countries — Sweden, Finland, Denmark, Germany. The two travelers met many people during their trip. One person Siikavaara met was the president of a company that encourages exchange students between America and Sweden. Just by chance, the president of the organization from America would be arriving in a few days. Would he greet her?

Siikavaara agreed. He and the friend met her, gave her a ride with a reindeer and presented her with a reindeer coat. The woman was overwhelmed by the kindness and attention. She asked Siikavaara, "Who are you?"

He quipped, "Why, I'm the midnight sun sheriff of Pajala."

The name stuck and now, should you meet Siikavaara, you get a business card. On one side is the name of his guest ranch. On the other side is a color portrait of the policeman in cowboy hat and fringed leather reindeer jacket and pants. The midnight sun is behind him, a knife in its sheath at this side. His arms are folded. He's the midnight sun sheriff of Pajala.

I first met Siikavaara a few days earlier in Kolari, Finland at the Arctic Canoe Race. The computer was out and plugged into an outlet at a campground. This was my outdoor office, in the shade, out of the hot August, Arctic sun. A large shadow quickly formed and I looked up into the light. There was a man, dressed in leather fringe, on a horse, just maybe a foot or so from where I was sitting.

He said something to me. I didn't understand. Maybe it was Finnish or it could have been Swedish. He switched to English and the confusion was lessened.

"What are you doing?," he asked.

I explained my journey.

He reached into the pocket of his reindeer coat and pulled out a business card and it floated down to where I was seated.

"You are welcome," he said.

Then he rode off to perform a few riding tricks for the crowd.

A few days later I was in Siikavaara's kitchen, listening to his stories, learning about the knife and watching him go through scrapbooks filled with newspaper clippings and photos of himself. There he is shooting partridge from horseback. There he is again, riding his horse with Miss Sweden in 1994. There he is again, with a huge horse trailer just purchased from America.

The stories go on and on.

Ranch Siikavaara is located about 20 miles west of Pajala at the end of a road that rolls along farmland where hay was being harvested on a sleepy Sunday morning.

There is a sign and a road that leads up to the ranch. On this Sunday morning, Siikavaara, dressed in shorts and short-sleeved shirt, was leading two women and a girl on a ride around the ranch.

At first he didn't recognize the rider on the bicycle. Then he did and quickly switched to English.

"Take a look around," he said as he guided the trio on horseback.

The ranch covers about 2,000 acres and has three lakes. It has been in the family since 1886. On it is the house with Western-style memorabilia everywhere. Horns are on every wall it seemed, some draped with holsters, others with saddles. In the kitchen is a painting of Siikavaara, done by a friend, Leena Teån. Cabins and a couple of Sami-sytle tents are on the property. Down by one of the lakes is a sauna and a floating bath. Made out of wood and steel drums, there is a stove on the floating tub. The bath is filled with water, the stove lit and you have an outdoor bathing experience for the whole family. There are stables and about a dozen horses. Trails encircle the property. The plump blueberries were ripe for picking. Four white Arctic hare darted across the path. Two big horn sheep from Corsica were fenced off, plus a few deer. He also had pigs.

He called one big, black ugly porker a "Canadian mini-pig." The big hog startled me. At first, I didn't quite know what it was. So ugly, its face squashed in, it looked blind. Did it have eyes? It certainly had a flat snout and was sniffing around. I reached down to touch it. The spine of bristles was rough to the touch. The creature looked more like a brush to clean the grill on a barbecue than swine. The pig now followed me around as I took a tour of the ranch.

One of the three riders included Leena; friend, writer, radio personality, painter and singer. We chatted outside, drinking coffee, eating bread with butter and jam, meat and eggs. Afterwards, we went into the kitchen and Åke (pronounced oakie), pulled down the scrapbooks and the stories began.

The "midnight sun sheriff of Pajala," Åke Siikavaara, leads one of his horses out to pasture at his ranch in Sweden.

He was born in Pajala 49 years ago. Divorced, his three children lived in Stockholm. He moved to Stockholm and worked as a police officer there for 18 years, before returning to the roots of his family's farm in Pajala. A year later he opened the guest ranch for riding, adventures into the woods and corral hunting.

Siikavaara is a well-traveled man, using contacts through an international police association to see parts of the United States and Canada. He has bagged both Alaskan grizzly and black bears. He has visited the Rocky Mountains of Canada and hunted puma in Arizona. He has navigated down the Colorado River and through the Grand Canyon. In 1977, he and two other Swedish policeman rode on horseback from Valdez, Alaska to Dawson City in the Canadian Yukon. He has also driven down the West Coast's famous ocean highway.

Now his days are spent on patrol in Pajala. He doesn't ride his horse or wear his reindeer skins. He wears your basic blue and drives a Volvo in the summer and patrols on snow machine in the winter.

At the kitchen table, he boosts that the Torne valley has the lowest crime rate in the world. They don't use locks here.

Well, there is one lock, the Torne valley lock.

"The Torne valley lock. You take a broom and put it against the door. No keys," he says. "That's how they lock the doors here."

There are problems. Suicide is an issue in these parts, particularly among single, unemployed men of all ages. A lot of what the police force in a 5,000 square mile area does is combat drinking and driving. They clean up after a suicide. They look after poachers who hunt and fish illegally. The woods are filled with moose and reindeer. There are collisions between these animals and autos. The police take care of these too.

Not much drugs, he said, but there is alcoholism. They are called to break up family disputes and fights in restaurants.

One day Siikavaara will retire, and he wants to make his living in the tourism business.

All sorts come to his ranch. That summer, he hosted about 500 people for a country and western jamboree, complete with bull-riding and ax-throwing. On his kitchen table was a CD from a country and western band from California that had heard about the festival. They wanted to come and play there. He still had the American flag up at the entrance of the ranch, welcoming the revelers with a touch of western flair.

From all over Europe, they come. They also come from further away, like South Africa and Australia, to hunt. Hunters have big money and they will pay handsomely for a trophy. Northern Sweden may not have grizzlies or tigers or lions, but it does have reindeer.

"They want to hunt reindeer and have a trophy. The hunters come from all over the world. They want to come and shoot a reindeer. It is a new experience," he said.

The area is also home to brown bear. If anything, Siikavaara is not short of ideas. He had this idea for people to get married. But it should be in some unusual place. He began to arrange for couples to get married in bear dens. Of course, this had to be during the summer when the bears weren't home.

The dens aren't very big. There isn't enough room for the whole wedding party, just the bride and groom. The priest and the rest of the party stand outside the den while the bride and groom crawl in. Of course, Siikavaara got press for this. He also manufactured some amusing photos. Imagine a hole in the ground and all you see are people's feet sticking out of the hole, in a missionary position.

"People think I'm crazy. Sometimes I do things that are a little crazy," he admitted.

This has also gotten him the label as "Sweden's craziest policeman." That's what was on the cover of a somewhat risqué magazine called *Aktuell Rapport* in 1992. Inside is the sheriff, in his western gear on a horse and also in his police blues in Pajala.

Perhaps some of the business savvy has been passed down to Siikavaara from his father. His father was the first in the area to export reindeer horns to Japan, China and Vietnam in the 1950s for their apparent aphrodisiac qualities.

Siikavaara, remember a local policeman, now makes spoons out of the reindeer antlers and grinds down the horns into a powder. The powder can be made into a pill, that when consumed, is thought to enhance the potency of males. Of course, Siikavaara has to put on a show. He sometimes takes visitors out to a cabin by a spring where he makes the powder, and beats a drum and chants, creating a bit of mystique and shamanism around the practice. He also sells the powder with spoon in pouches.

As to whether it works, he doesn't say. He does have a regular customer, a Danish doctor, who orders about a pound of the powder from him every year, and has for about the past 10 years.

"I think it is for her husband, " he says.

The sheriff is part of Siikavaara's image as he tries to sell Pajala as a place to visit. He wants to turn it into "Mecca like for the Muslims." Though Siikavaara could possibly be the area's most famous present day resident, it also was home to Lars Levi Læstadius, who some call a prophet. He lived from 1800 to 1861 and started his own religion. He was known as a revival preacher, temperance protagonist, scientist and botanist. He was ordained as a priest in 1826 in Karesuando. Then after 20 years there, he lived in Pajala until he died. Siikavaara wants to turn Pajala and the area into a place for the followers, to come and see where their leader lived and died.

For now, the policeman also rides in television commercials. Just that summer his friend Leena released a CD with a song called "Tornedalen Travolta" which tells about Siikavaara and his potent reindeer powder. There is also a song on the CD where the sheriff makes his debut as a songwriter.

Perhaps one day a country and western song in English will be written about the midnight sun sheriff of Pajala.

And as for how much he paid for that knife, he isn't saying. But he is saying it was worth its weight not in gold, but in international public relations.

CHAPTER TWENTY-FIVE

Strange English, Strange Coffee

I like Swedish fish. The fish is a sweet and chewy candy shaped like fish. My favorite is red. Being in Sweden, I thought it would be a perfect place to hook one.

But the first Swedish fish I tasted was salmon, grilled roadside by a couple of anglers. Northern Sweden is blessed with some fine fishing. They've also set up public cabins and picnic areas where anglers can gut, clean and cook their catch not far from the river the fish used to swim.

I stopped by one of these roadside oases during my first few miles into the country. The idea was to rest. Two men sat at a fire, cooking something up. They said a few words in Swedish to me. I answered in English. They spoke English, and the familiar round of questions began.

They were grilling something wrapped in tin foil and said they were on a fishing holiday. They were having quite the holiday. They showed me a white bucket. Inside was fish.

It was salmon they had caught in the morning. They were grilling the fish.

They had plenty of fish and wondered if I wanted some.

Yes, please, I answered.

I watched first how they ate the fish, peeling off the skin and then pulling the meat from the bone with their fingers. They had cups nearby to wash their fingers as the scales and skin can get sticky. The skin and bones then went into the fire.

They used the words trout and salmon interchangeably in describing the fish. But I think it was a river salmon and a fish called char. The foil had a spice laced in, like a smoked flavor. The two also had salted the fish. Some of the most simple things are the best things and the taste of fresh fish grilled over birch was one of them. Throw in fresh spring water tasting like champagne and the meal was complete. The two urged me to eat as much as I wanted. I did. They were a bit tired of the fish as they had been eating just this simple diet for a few days.

Not me. This was a new taste, not one of pasta or cold cuts or cheese. I pulled off the skin, each time getting less sloppy, and plucked the cooked meat from the bone.

They saw my delight. They would have to throw the fish out that wasn't eaten. Would I like some?

I certainly didn't want to take any to cook, so they threw six salmon on the grill and cooked them up for me to take. This perhaps was the finest welcome I could have asked for into Sweden. There is nothing like a bicyclist carrying a six-pack of fish.

Swedish fish was just one example of strange foods and strange English I encountered during the ride. Though reindeer and herring was sampled, so was a Tornedalen Sunday tradition, though I had it on a Monday. It was something called cheese in the coffee.

I don't know much about how this culinary tradition started, but I did read about it somewhere and mentioned it to Åke Siikavaara when I was at his ranch in Sweden. He had some of the cheese. It was a white cheese and had the consistency of tofu. It had somewhat of a rubbery feel and taste. I put in only two cubes of the cheese. I watched as Åke put in a handful of the curd and a teaspoon of sugar. I followed suit.

You eat the cheese with a teaspoon. I can't say I'll become a regular, but it was a novelty to add to the list of different foods I've tried during this trip.

Though in a few minutes, my stomach had rebelled against my adventurous taste buds. I can say I returned the tradition to the very earth that had born it.

Not only did I encounter strange foods, but strange sights too. I did a double take when I saw a three-wheeled car. I also did a double take when I saw a couple of German cyclists carrying reindeer antlers in their gear. It became even more amazing when I saw they also were carrying juggling pins.

Strange English also followed me near and above the circle. The first outrageous use of it, that made me really take notice, was in Iceland at a campground when a Jacuzzi was referred to as a "hot pot with pressure."

I certainly don't want to make fun of anyone who attempts English as a second language, as I've been looked at rather strangely for my attempts at foreign languages. For example, I was once working as a radio reporter in Israel during the late 1980s. My Hebrew and Arabic were, and still are, pathetic. Instead, I relied on English-speaking resources. One day I got a call from the assignment desk in New York telling me I'm to do a story about police encouraging the use of condoms among prostitutes as a way to combat AIDS. Using crack journalistic expertise, I found out that prostitutes frequent a section of a Tel Aviv beach. Armed with my tape recorder, I headed down to the beach. Not having a car, I opted to take a bus that day.

Every bus driver in Israel speaks English, except for the driver I had that day.

I got on the bus, paid my fare and sat behind the driver. The bus continued its route.

I asked the driver, in English, to tell me when we got to the beach. But he didn't understand.

So, I now had to try and ask this man where I could find the prostitutes. Of course, I had no idea what the Hebrew word was for prostitute.

In my attempt, I came up with the question: "Where are the women who want money for sex?"

He didn't seem phased by such a question, just answering in Hebrew with the word for "soon." After asking such a question on a public bus with many other passengers, one develops a certain paranoia as the bus driver started a conversation with a few of the passengers. It was only my imagination that one or two of them pointed at me.

He told me when we reached the stop. I got out and it wasn't long before I found a couple of English-speaking prostitutes who agreed to do an interview.

After recording their insights on tape, I was back at the bus stop.

The bus came. It stopped.

I got in.

It was the same driver.

"So, how was it?," he asked.

I became redder than the desert sun, and quite flustered, as I tried to explain in poor, pigeon Hebrew that I was merely a journalist on assignment. I went so far as to show the driver my press card.

So I certainly can appreciate those who try to speak a language they haven't mastered.

I also love seeing and hearing it, because it can be damn funny.

In Norway, I saw a sign on a ferry. It read: "Naked flames prohibited." I thought how discriminatory this was. Everyone should be allowed aboard, clothed or not.

Lakselv, Norway is a small town on the shores of a fjord. It was a point, after the ride down from the North Cape, where I was to say good-bye to the sea for awhile before heading inland to Karasjok. It's also where I said good-bye to a pain in my butt.

Literally.

Sometime after the visit to the top of Europe, I developed an inflamed hemorrhoid. I won't go into many details here, but riding with a painful swelling in the netherworld is like trying to get comfortable while sitting on the blade of an extremely sharp knife. Let's just say each bump in the road became an adventure.

Pharmacies were rare along the coastal road, and it wasn't until I reached Lakselv that I found one. Once I found it, the question remained as to how as I was going to explain my problem. I thought a little show and tell might get the job done, but it might also lead to my arrest.

So, I had to come up with the least amount of words in English to describe my malady to someone who might not understand.

I decided I could best sum up my problem with one word and one letter of the English alphabet.

I walked inside. The woman behind the counter looked at me and said something.

I smiled and answered, "Preparation H."

The woman stared blankly and shrugged.

Once again, I said the magic words, this time gesturing with my right index finger to the afflicted area.

The woman also projected an index finger in response, motioning for me to wait.

She returned with a co-worker who asked in English if she could help me.

I smiled and said, "Preparation H."

"Please write down," she said and handed me a piece of paper and pen. I returned the paper with the name of the medicine. She went back to a computer and apparently entered a search for the over-the-counter remedy. She returned with a tube of rectal salve.

This certainly was the strangest use of the English language I had ever encountered.

Oh, the ointment worked.

Then there was a sign in a Karasjok, Norway youth hostel. It said: "After the rules of the Youth Hostel Fuderation, do all our guests have to tidy and clean before they leave!"

So, was that a statement or a question?

Though my journey into Russia was but a mere few hours, I did catch a couple of charming quotes from the tour guide. Each time we went into

A six-pack of freshly caught Swedish fish is prepared at a rest area.

a different section of a Murmansk museum, she would turn to us and say, "Welcome to this hall." It was sweet the first time, cute the second time and a bit annoying by the third time.

When we finished the tour, she thanked each of us by saying, "Thank you for being my tourist."

I said, you're welcome.

Before going back aboard the boat to Norway, we passed through customs in Murmansk. A section was roped off. There was a sign in English which discouraged visitors from venturing there. But it didn't say do not enter. Instead, the sign said, "no to go."

Finland has some good guffaws too. In the Kolari campground where I stumbled across the Arctic Canoe Race there were signs on the doors to the toilets. They did not say vacant or occupied. One side said "free." Flip it over and it said, "no free."

Finland was also a place with stunning log homes by the road. Outside of Inari, I took a look around a company which manufactured these homes and picked up an English-language brochure. It said: "The old, sturdy flat-topped pine is colled aihki. The share of the red heartwood is most nearly 70 percent. Aihki logs are suitable especially for the building of the greats and impressives buildings."

There was also one from a Finnish government pamphlet about "Everyman's right in Finland." Right there on page seven was advice for people who want to search for mushrooms. "Remember that mushroom picking can be dangerous; make sure you are well-infirmed before picking any."

My favorite was in a brochure I picked up at a campground, which was lauding its log cottages by the river. "By the rapids of Kaamasjoki there are two bungalows of deadwood," it stated. "In these bungalows an original cottage atmosphere is combined with modern conveniences. The relaxing effect of deadwood is amazing, you can really feel it in those bungalows."

CHAPTER TWENTY-SIX

The Hotel That Wasn't

In the summer, the most famous attraction in Jukkasjårvi isn't there. Well, it is, sort of, but you really have to use your imagination. I was camped right next to it and didn't even really see it. Though I really did see it as I looked out onto the river. Except what I wanted to see was a part of the Baltic Sea by now.

Yngve Bergqvist would have just laughed at my predicament. When you live 125 miles above the Arctic Circle in Sweden you are, by nature, a winter person. Yet every summer, there are days when visitors pop in and ask the inevitable question: "So, where is it?"

You see, Bergqvist owns it. He, or a member of his staff, will just look at you, and probably laugh inside, and point to the river and say, "It was there."

Come October, construction will begin again. First the snow blowers will come and start mixing in the manmade snow with the natural snow. Then huge plows will push the tons of snow onto a frame. The frame will be taken away and eventually, 4,000 tons of snow and ice will become the world's biggest igloo and a 12-room ice hotel.

Not only can you sleep on an ice bed with reindeer skins in a sleeping bag while the temperature hovers in the 20s inside, you can try the indoor golf range, belly-up to the ice bar where the glasses are made of ice and every drink is made on the rocks (beer bottles and cans are wrapped in reindeer skin to prevent freezing), watch a movie on chairs carved of ice,

The man who designed the ice hotel in Jukkasjärvi, Sweden, Yngve Bergqvist, takes summer visitors on a tour via his computer.

take a sauna on ice-blocks (imagine how a popsicle feels), view the art galleries to see jewel-like sculptures, get married in the chapel, climb one of the 90 foot-high pillars or try the ice challenge rope course. Of course, should this not be enough for you, you can always sign up for a survival course with Bergqvist and learn how to fish, trap ptarmigan and make pine tea.

The idea of making a hotel out of ice came during a vodka-induced sauna session. Bergqvist and some friends were yearning for their childhood days of building snow caves and snow forts. Someone suggested building a hotel. In 1990, it became a reality. Now, each year, visitors from around the world make the trip to the ice hotel, paying $200 a night (double occupancy) to sleep, if they can, on ice.

Truly, the ice hotel is an environmentalists dream. It is biodegradable. Each year in May, it starts to melt away to make room for river rafters and fishermen who come to hook salmon, trout, grayling and Arctic char. The hotel isn't big by hospitality industry standards, but huge for blocks of ice thrown together. It is some 3,600 square feet, with a frame 18 feet high and 18 feet wide. Water is sprayed on it to hold it together. It is entirely made of snow and ice. Well, a part of the sauna is made of wood.

"Normally, people see snow as a problem. It's on the roof, you have to shovel it. It's in the way," said Bergqvist. "You could make a garage or a stable for a horse. You could use snow for many things, especially during the colder periods. It insulates. The temperature can be 25 degrees warmer inside than outside."

In the summer, the ice hotel leaves much to the imagination. Just gaze out onto the river and picture it frozen. Close your eyes and see a legion of people, clad in one-piece snow suits with animal skin hats, arriving on skis, snowmobiles, reindeer-pulled sled, horse-drawn sled, dog sled, snowshoes and on horseback during a 10 mile trek from the airport in Kiruna (about a 90 minute flight from Stockholm).

"Bicycle?," said Bergqvist. "No, they don't come by bicycle in the winter. Try to bike when it's 25 degrees below zero (centigrade)."

No thanks. I'd rather splash around the river in summer and think I waded through a bit of that winter's hotel.

CHAPTER TWENTY-SEVEN

Nick's Lake

Hikers would be more inclined to visit a tiny place called Nikkaluokta than any bicyclist. Merely a blip on a map, the village is about 40 miles west of the mining town of Kiruna. The village is situated at the end of the road. Literally, where Nikkaluokta begins, the road ends. That means for bicyclists, the road in is also the road out.

But for hikers, Nikkaluokta is an oasis. It is a stop on the approximately 300 mile long *Kungsluden* or King's Way trail. The trail winds through northern Sweden, including a route up Kebnekaise, the country's highest peak at 6,973 feet.

Nikkaluokta is little more than a valley rest station. There are about a dozen or so homes. There aren't really streets, but paths that are best traveled in winter by snow machines or skis. There's a church, cabins, campground and lodge. Inside the lodge is a small store. Here, hikers can rest up from one of the treks, like the seven-day, 65 mile hike to Abisko National Park.

Plump blueberries wait to be picked. The soft light of late day falls on trees which even in August are starting to turn color. Sometimes a helicopter flys above.

Nikkaluokta called out to me. Not because of the hiking, though that could be a trip for another time. Northern Sweden had become a tad uneventful heading into mid-August. Already, the traveling season was shutting down and though the calendar said summer, the feeling was more like late fall. The twin towns of Gällivare and Malmbarget are known for their mining histories and winter sports. Malmbarget was once Sweden's Klondike and rapid growth turned it at one time into a hideous shantytown. Tours into the local mine had already ceased for the summer and the shantytown had closed its doors the day before I arrived.

Gällivare was pleasant enough with its downtown benches, fountains and flowers, but what tore me up was going to the new fly-fishing museum and finding displays only in Swedish. The recommendation came from a person who knew I spoke only English. However, one must find some good, and I'm happy to say I learned that fly-fishing legend Abu Garcia was actually a Swede and not the brother of the late Grateful Dead leader Jerry Garcia.

That's a joke.

Northern Sweden was filled with forest and dale, lakes and rivers. It also has a small city, called Kiruna. Founded at the turn of the century, Kiruna became the world's largest underground mine. The city has a church, which looks like a Sami *kåta*, and a magnificent city hall with a sculpted clock tower. Visiting city hall, one feels as though they are in an art museum with paintings, statues and exhibits. Mining money has flowed into its halls. Also, it was a city with bike paths (many northern towns have them), and traffic lights for cyclists.

But in Kiruna, I learned about a man named Enoch Sarri. A Sami, he was known throughout Sweden as a weather prognasticator. Except he had some rather unusual ways to predict the days ahead. He would project his forecast by examining the contents of reindeer and fish bellies. This was a man I wanted to meet.

The road to Nikkaluokta passed the large iron mine. Young motorcross riders growled around a dirt track further on. Small homes were hidden in the woods. Every once in a while a person or two would be by the side of the road, holding a bucket filled with freshly picked cloudberries. The road pavement changed from time to time, giving the impression it was built in sections. It was. The whole road to Nikkaluokta wasn't constructed until 1971. Before then, a boat brought visitors. Others would drive their cars on the ice in winter.

The silence would be broken by reindeer grazing by the roadside. I would stop. We would stare at each other. I would proceed and eventually they would seek camouflage in the forests.

Golden fields, tall green grass waving in the wind and glistening lakes welcome the visitor to the end of the road. On a clear day, snow-capped peaks can be seen.

Though there isn't much in Nikkaluokta, chances are you will run into a Sarri. When you pay for a camping site, a Sarri will take your money.

When you pick up some pasta at the store, a Sarri will be behind the register. Who knows? A Sarri might even be in the store doing some shopping too.

The Sarris have been running the village for nearly 100 years. That's because they founded it.

Nilsolsson and Maria Sarri were a couple of reindeer herders around the turn of the century. Each year they herded the reindeer from area to area, near the Norwegian border in summer and then down into the woods near Pajala in winter. But one winter, the herd died.

"This could be the story of any Sami family in any valley," said Anna Sarri, a direct descendent of Nilsolsson and Maria. "Our grandmother and grandfather, they lost their reindeer during a bad year. The reindeer died. They settled down. They got a whole bunch of children. They started to fish and hunt and try tourism."

Anna Sarri knows a bit about tourism. She is one of the handful of Sarris running the lodge in Nikkaluokta. Another Sarri who helped run things was Yvla Sarri who with Anna, provided me with a short history of the family.

Nilsolsson and Maria decided to stay in the valley by the lake. They named it Nikkaluokta which translates to "Nick's lake." The founding couple begat 14 children. Those 14 begat 22. Those 22 were working on more that summer.

Anna and Yvla were sitting on the second floor of the wood lodge, built in 1988. Scores of years earlier Nilsolsson and Maria started to take in travelers. The wealthy and well-known of Sweden used to come to the area to trek and explore the foothills of the country's highest peak. They needed a place to stay.

"People came and they started to take people in," said Anna. "The first time they took guests into their home, gave them food and a place to stay overnight. When the children grew up, they said it was not bad to take some payment."

Yvla continued, "That's the way hospitality started here. That's why we are here now. We are third generation living off of tourism."

It was their Uncle Enoch, one of the 14 children of Nilsolsson and Maria, who started to put Nikkaluokta on the map.

Enoch was well-versed in the traditions of Sami culture. He was a reindeer herder like his father. Each fall, during the slaughter of the reindeer, Enoch would cut open a few other carcasses to examine what they had been eating.

"All different cultures have ways to mark how the weather is coming. You can see it in the clouds, in the trees, in the animals," said Anna.

"We can't give you all the answers. We can't speak for our uncle, but he did take care of the old ways to know about the weather," said Yvla.

Enoch would see what the reindeer and fish he caught had been eating. He was seeing how they were preparing for the upcoming weather.

According to the contents, Enoch would then make a prediction about the upcoming weather. He was a bit of a living Swedish "Farmer's Almanac".

Word spread about Enoch's prediction. Nikkaluokta is situated in an area which has some of the country's coldest temperatures. The rest of Sweden was interested in the weather at the base of the mighty mountain. Weather services in Stockholm would call him for weather observations. So before a weather station was set up in the remote village and before the advent of computers, Enoch became the area weatherman and notariety followed.

"As time went by, he found out that people were interested in Nikkaluokta," said Anna. "I think he came up that this was a good way for tourism and to get Nikkaluokta known. In his best year, he was in all the Swedish newspapers. We still get questions. People want to know if he is here and what he says the weather will be."

Enoch, and his five brothers, still resided in the village their father founded. He wasn't there the day Anna and Yvla were being questioned.

I never met him. He's also old, and doesn't make the predictions any more, I was told.

To get an idea of how old the Sarri story is, Anna and Yvla opened up a scrapbook. The children of Nilsolsson and Maria Sarri had their own lives and went their own ways. In 1962, Maria died. The children all met in Nikkaluokta for the family. There a photo was taken of all the children. On August 24 of that year, the photo appeared in a newspaper. Why? The ages of all 14 children totaled over 1,000 years.

In these days of divorce, separation, one-parent families, families stretched acrosss the world, birth control and abortion, it's hard to imagine 14 long-lasting children coming together for one purpose, even their mother's funeral.

"In the Sami way of thinking, the family is important," said Anna. "They stay together. Family is family. It's not so strange."

The Sarri children don't go to school in Nikkaluokta. There isn't one. Instead, they are educated in Kiruna. They don't come home everyday as the long, dark winters would make the commute unbearable. They stay in Kiruna.

Around mid-September, the Sarris shut down their operations until March. It's dark. It's cold. It's even too cold to go cross-country skiing. It's a quiet time. A time for introspection, and a time to stay indoors. There are only a few hours of daylight.

But in late fall, they still return to their roots. Though only 10 percent of the Sami are still reindeer herders, there are those herders who call on their relatives to help during round-up time.

"Sometimes they need people to help them with their reindeer, to catch them, to mark them and so on. Then they call their relatives and ask for their help," said Yvla.

"It's hard work, but it's fun. It's more than fun. It's like what your ancestors did way back," said Anna.

With so much opportunity in the rest of the world, it's a bit hard to fathom how one family can live at the end of the road for so long. But Anna is quick to answer why she stays.

"It's easy," she said. "Look outside. You see the mountains. I feel strong here because of my family and because of the mountains."

CHAPTER TWENTY-EIGHT

Beginning Of The End

It wasn't raining inside the restaurant at the Riksgränsen ski area. The slopes were brown, but it felt as though snow could fall at any minute. The past couple of days had been miserable, weatherwise. One German cyclist said it was like November in his country. But the calendar read August 20.

Riksgränsen is barely in Sweden. If you know how, you can ski the backcountry by taking a lift in Sweden and finish up the run in Norway.

It is one of the northernmost ski areas in the world and has a reputation where you can ski mid-summer in the midnight sun. But the slopes had been closed since the end of June, and even then, ponds and lakes in the rugged mountains still had ice clinging to the surfaces.

The shortest summer I had ever experienced had ended and autumn was coming in with the speed of a bullet. The mountainous border region had whiteouts caused by fog. Clouds dipped down near the road. The leaves were losing their green and bob houses stacked near lake shores seemed to inch closer to the waters which eventually freeze to support ice anglers and snow machines. Even with the dampness and clouds, the E-10 roadway was one of the most stunning parts of Sweden I saw. That is, except for the blondes.

A sense of melancholy overwhelmed me. Ever since leaving Nikkaluokta, I felt the beginning of the end. Soon, the road would lead back to Narvik, Norway and the second of two circles would be completed.

The road went back to Kiruna, and then on to Narvik, along a road which had only opened in 1984. The route led to the tiny Abisko National Park, perched on the shores of the long lake Torneträsk. The climb was back up to the clouds where the land was sprinkled with the previous season's snow and the lake mirrored the mountains.

Since Kiruna, rain came by for a visit and decided to stay. The temperature hovered in the 50s and discomfort crept in. Beauty is hard to see when you are miserable, but I tried.

When the cold and wet proved too much to take, I headed indoors where possible, like to the restaurant at Riksgränsen. I was in time for the buffet lunch.

The beginning of the end signals a time to reminisce about the journey, even though it has not yet ended. I looked out at the grayness through the nearly deserted dining room and stuck a piece of herring in my mouth. Fish, I had never eaten so much fish before in my life. There was fish in cans, fish in tins and fish in a tube. I ate tuna, salmon, char, grayling, dried fish, fish that had been filleted, pickled herring, herring in tomato sauce, herring in dill, herring in Thousand Island dressing, pepper mackerel, mackerel in tomato sauce and caviar. There I was in the Land of Great Smoked Fish, where the cream cheese flowed, and there wasn't a decent bagel for a thousand miles.

I had eaten reindeer of all kinds — soup, chops and pate´. I had gone through various phases of nourishment. At times, I just ate sausage. I didn't eat many ramen noodles, as pasta with crushed tomatoes became the main staple. For dinner, there was rice and beans, beans and pasta, pasta and tomato sauce, pasta, tomato sauce and tuna fish, and pasta and mackerel. Lunch was an assortment of open face sandwiches of cheese and cold cuts while breakfast could have been milk and cereal, bread and cheese, bread and jam, and bread and chocolate spread. Yogurt entered the diet too. For snacks, I stuck to peanuts and raisins. Though large European chocolate bars had a way of seducing me from time to time.

I had cycled roads that didn't have huge campers hogging the pavement. I had seen three-wheeled cars, and a driver in a Mercedes-Benz actually pulling a camper. These vehicles didn't have license plates like in America with snappy slogans which read "Live Free or Die" or "The Best Snow on Earth." They just had simple numbers and a letter which designated their country. Most could be figured out. Sweden has the letter S, while Denmark was DK. Norway was just an N while Finland was FIN. Germany was D and France was F. NL was the Netherlands and Poland had a PL. Italy was an I and Russia an R. Switzerland was a CH. But there was one that I couldn't figure out — SF. One day I learned it too stood for Finland. Finnish people called their country *Suomi*. But in Finland some joke the SF stands for Soviet Finland.

I had been totally dirty. I had gone from a life of wearing different clothes every day, to wearing the same clothes every day — for a week. The same socks stayed on the same putrid feet for six or seven days straight. The same shirt would be peeled off the sweat-coated skin after three days. Clean clothes weren't really clean. They were just clothing I hadn't worn for a few days and when I put them on, they gave the illusion of clean.

Though my foreign language skills are poor because of lack of effort, I was forced to learn a few words. Cycling through Finland, I figured it was a country of big drinkers. There were sections of towns where storefronts had huge banners with the word *ale* written across them. This was not an advertisement for an alcoholic beverage. The word *ale* means sale in Finnish.

In Sweden, the doors taught me a new word. It only took one or two knocks in the face to learn that *drag* meant pull.

There is no drug like travel, I thought. Perhaps that is a drug to which I will forever be addicted. Nothing matches its high. But there are doses and strengths in which it can be consumed. The key is to find a balance to satisfy oneself.

That is something I will have to experiment with, I thought during a second trip to the buffet to fill up my plate with herring, rice, bread and cheese.

Then again, taking the argument that I am sort of addict, perhaps there is a cure. Maybe I can't function with my addiction.

Therefore, perhaps I should have some sort of program to rid me of my desire to travel. So I jotted down a few things:

1. Get rid of any books that may inspire adventure like "Travels with Charlie," "Zen and the Art of Motorcycle Maintenance" and "Walk Across America."

2. Cancel subscription to "National Geographic" and any other travel-related periodicals.

3. Burn any maps and atlases.

4. Don't have a credit card which rewards use with free airline tickets.

5. Refrain from drinking imported beer. That only encourages a dream to visit the brewery. That can also be applied to imported wine and vineyard tours. Come to think of it, scotch whiskey too.

6. Only frequent burger-producing fast-food restaurants. This will deaden taste buds and squash any desire to visit another country because of its food.

7. Have name removed from mailing list of every gear and equipment

catalog.

8. Wear electronic collar that emits excruciating pain when wearer travels over 100 miles from home.

9. Marry a woman who suffers from fear of flying and car-sickness.

10. Get a real job with only one or two weeks of vacation per year.

But I planned none of these drastic measures. Instead, I paid for my meal, set up camp at a closed campground and spent the last night in my tent listening to the Swedish rain lull me to sleep.

CHAPTER TWENTY-NINE

Second Circle Completed

The beer was expensive, about $8, but alcohol is always ridiculously priced in Arctic Scandinavia. This beer was worth every cent. It was the beer to signify the end of the road.

Sliding into one of the pub chairs was welcomed. The warmth wrapped itself around me with the surrounding cigarette smoke.

Into the glass I peered, maybe hoping to see replays of the three month, 3,002 mile journey I had just completed. Magically, the light-bodied beverage became like a movie screen for my memories and in it I saw a figure on a bicycle in the rain.

For the last three days, the rain had not given up. It choose different forms of attack from a light mist to a relentless downpour as the road went from Sweden back into Norway, over mountains not fully seen because of the fog and clouds. It was home to the snow that never leaves.

Even in August, came the smell of birch. There is plenty of birch at the top of Europe. Birch to light a summer woodstove. Birch to grill fresh fish and birch to get the sauna fired up. For me, I will always be transported back to this place by the sweet smell of white wood.

The rain had won and soaked a tent that had mistakenly been placed in an area that turned into a swamp overnight. That happened in Riksgränsen, where the tent was transformed into an indoor swimming pool. The sleeping pad kept the body somewhat dry, but when it is wet inside and wet outside you know you're in for a dreary day.

Luckily, this happened only 40 miles from Narvik, the city where the second circle was completed.

Only a few hours more to a dry hostel and the end of a journey. The road reached high into the mountains. Trees were scant. The border crossing wasn't even a formality. In a second, Sweden became Norway. Communities, perhaps the second homes of many living in Narvik, sprouted up on the rocks. The road dipped and the muscles ached to climb yet another tough Norwegian incline. The road swung low and the reward was effortless passage.

There was the sea again. The route was the E-6, the most unpleasant road of the whole journey. By Narvik, it is narrow, winding and filled with a stream of oh-so-close vehicles.

There was Narvik again, a city with both beauty in its hills and an ugliness from the mining operations which support it.

This was not a spiritual, mystical ride of self-enlightenment. Though whenever one travels for so long, that road will be walked upon, like it or not. No, quite simply, this was just a ride to see whose paths would cross.

There was one person I wanted to see, whose path I wanted to cross again, before heading into a pub for a bit of celebration. His name was Ronald Berg. Some two months before, the road had led to Narvik and to his Cycle, Ski and Surf Shop in the dirty industrial section of the city.

He had requested a postcard at my journey's end.

Instead, I went to thank him.

My bicycle was not perfect during the Arctic ride. I had to replace the rear tire along the way in Ivalo, Finland. I replaced the pedals in Kirkenes, Norway. Flats would only number two and a link in the chain had snapped in Iceland. However, the new bicycle broke at least one spoke in each country. Sometimes two spokes snapped off in a particular country for a total of seven on the rear wheel. On occasion, I was actually able to replace one or two. I was carrying emergency Kevlar-string spokes which even the mechanically-infirmed like myself can use.

It also meant a few stops in bike shops, like in Akureyri, Iceland. There, they had no bike stands. Instead, the bikes were hung from hooks in the ceiling and worked on. Other times, as in Gällivare, Sweden, I was charged a whopping $36 for replacement of two spokes. Bikers beware. Rip-offs await.

The majority of workers in bike shops were helpful, especially Berg. The clamps on my front rack were breaking easily, no doubt because I hadn't tightened them enough at the beginning of the trip. They were being held together with wire and duct tape. Replacements were hard to come by.

Berg looked at the bike. He went to look for the clamps.

"I like tourists because they have problems that make me think," he said, and then went to look for the proper clamps. He didn't have any. However, this did not deter him.

He left the shop and returned with a metal strip. Right there, he fit and cut custom-made clamps for the rack.

"These I guarantee," he said.

Those are famous last words of many mechanics. I wanted Berg's words to be true.

They were.

So I returned to his shop, and thanked him.

Then it was short ride to the hostel where I checked in, and found a room downstairs to dry out all the wet equipment I had.

The weather was starting to clear. Soon, school children, who return to school in August were let from their lessons and filled the city streets. The slopes of the ski area came into view. I found a pub near the bus station and just got lost in my head.

So many other memories swirled in the liquid in the Land of the Midnight Herring. The other night I saw my first Arctic star through a brief clearing. The midnight sun was beginning to fade from its pulpit, and a sort of normalcy was returning to the night sky. But normal is hard to define here, for in weeks, the moon would take the stage and stay for quite some time during the northern polar nights with the aurora borealis as dancers.

I would not see this winter drama though. It was time to head back. My money belt, that ever-present ground to home which housed my important documents, swelled like a drawer at the exchange windows. Inside were currencies from four countries, the places I had cycled — Iceland, Norway, Finland and Sweden. Also there was my passport, with a stamp of Murmansk, Russia, a souvenir from a day I discovered a spin on the "no limits" philosophy of many an adventurer. I had found a way, unfortunately, to "know limits."

There in the bar, I raised the glass to my lips, and to no one in particular, drank a toast to life.

EPILOGUE

Going Home

The shortest distance between Narvik and home would have been to hire a private jet from Narvik to Portland, Maine and then engage a limo for the 70 mile drive home.

That would have been the easiest.

It didn't turn out that way. Instead, it took 11 hours by boat, 18 hours by train, 17 hours waiting for the bicycle at the train station, nearly eight hours on a plane and then a three hour car ride to get home.

Of course, all this was done in the same clothing.

The first part of this odyssey was the jaunt, by boat, from Narvik back to the Lofoten Islands and Svolvær. At the harbor, I transferred from a ferry to the M/S Lofoten, a floating time piece. The vessel is a member of the Coastal Express fleet which transports passengers between Bergen in southern Norway and Kirkenes. Each voyage calls on 34 ports and travels 2,500 nautical miles.

Without a cabin, I joined the other vagabonds in trying to catch a few hours of sleep in various uncomfortable curled-up positions on chairs in the lounge. Sleep is hard to come by, especially when your port, Bodø, is reached in the middle of the night. That was fine. The dock is a few hundred yards from the train station and the hostel is just on top of the station.

But, the hostel had closed for the night by the time the boat pulled in. It was dark now. I had no desire to check into a hotel for just a few hours. The train would come in the morning. Instead, I found a bench by the closed station, pulled out the sleeping bag, and caught a few winks there before two figures woke me. They were two backpackers. They too had found the hostel doors closed. They inquired if they could sleep there. No problem, I said. We were now three.

Judgment day came for the body bag. The oversized bag was left for nearly two months at the hostel. Would it still be there? I climbed the stairs to the spot where I had left it.

It was there, with a layer of dust covering it.

Nonetheless, it was usable.

I loaded all my gear into the bag, checked it and the bicycle, and got ready for the long, but pleasant train ride back to Oslo.

This time, the train went right through to the Norwegian capital. The last time I had been a passenger, we had to be taken off and bused for a distance. That didn't happen. The ride was smooth and beautiful.

The Oslo train station was familiar. Weeks before I had shared whiskey with a Dutch traveler. I went to claim my bike.

It wasn't there.

"On the next train," I was informed.

That wasn't a problem. So I walked around Olso for a while trying to get ready for my re-entry back into civilization. I hung out at the train station for a while, watching the busy bodies bustling through.

I went to check on the bike.

"On the next train," I was informed.

I started getting nervous. I explained I had a flight to catch. I asked them to call the station in Bodø to see if the bike had left. They did. They said the bike did leave. Where could it be? They said maybe Trondheim. Can you call Trondheim? They called Trondheim.

"On the next train," I was informed.

I wasn't the only anxious biker. There was another soul, a Frenchman named Michel. He had a flight too. He was nervous. He had been on the train down from Bodø. He was given the same saga.

The next train, unfortunately, was also the next day. We figured we would stay in the train station. The train station closes in the wee hours of the morning, we later found out.

We joined the motley crew of travelers, misfits and musicians who waited outside the closed doors until they would re-open again. Once the night clubs in the area started to close, their drunken patrons came to the station, expressed disgust it was closed, and then would try and catch some sleep on the pavement. What started as maybe a dozen people, easily tripled during the next few hours.

During the night, we were visited by a citizen patrol which offered coffee and snacks to those assembled on the pavement. They also offered rides to nearby hotels. Not one person accepted a ride. The coffee was popular though.

Daybreak came, the station re-opened and the smelly bunch headed inside to continue with their lives.

Michel and I went to the luggage claim area and hoped for the best. The train hadn't arrived yet, we were told.

We watched the arrival board. We saw it say the train had pulled in. Anxiously, we waited until the luggage was unloaded.

We returned.

There were the bikes and gear.

It had been a total of seventeen hours since arriving in Oslo. Bikes and bikers were re-united. Happiness reigned.

Oslo has an excellent array of bike paths. With a few hours to kill, Michel and I cycled around, visiting the Eidsvollsplass, a square between the parliament building and National Theater that is adorned with statues and fountains. Even in the early morning, tour guides were leading the herds on their on-the-bus, off-the-bus excursions.

Two more stops, via the bike paths, were made before Michel and I separated. First we stopped to explore the Fram, the polar schooner made famous in 1892 by explorer Fridtjof Nansen and then again in 1911 by Roald Amundsen. There was also a stop at the Kon-Tiki museum to see the papyrus reed boat Ra II, used by another famed Norwegian explorer, Thor Heyerdahl.

There, the Frenchman and I parted. It was an easy ride to the airport. But just about a mile from the entrance, a hissing sound snaked up to my ears from my rear tire, and the bike started to become sluggish. It was my second flat (the first one was in Finland), and my plane took off in just about two hours.

How ironic that the flat would happen so close to the end. But it was taken in good stride. The tube was easily replaced.

At the airport, the bike was handily placed on the plane. All I had to do was turn the handlebars and remove the pedals. No box, no plastic bag this time.

The flight first touched down in Iceland, where I loaded up on duty free items. Included in the purchases were the Icelandic schnapps, *Brennivin*, and a packet of hardfish. The flight continued onto Boston, and the final three hour car ride back north.

The *Brennivin,* hardfish, and a few tins of Norwegian mackerel in tomato sauce I purchased in Narvik are unusual souvenirs to bring back home. It was my intent to save them, until the day I finished writing about my summer above the circle.

On that day, I promised myself I would open them and share them. I would twist off the cap of the schnapps, cut open the hardfish and peel away the lid of the tinned mackerel. I would pour the *Brennivin* into shot glasses and say the words many a Scandinavian had said to me during my visit to their home — *God tur.*

Good tour, indeed.

April 13, 1997
Intervale, NH

ABOUT THE AUTHOR

Marty Basch is a writer whose articles have appeared in various newspapers and magazines across the United States and Canada. He has won several journalism awards for his reporting, and is the author of two books. He doesn't know exactly how many miles he has pedaled on a bicycle during his life, but he figures it is a lot. Basch lives somewhere in New Hampshire.

Against the Wind

A Maine to Alaska bicycling adventure
by Marty Basch

5,198 miles
116 days
10 flats
4 tires
2 chains
one grizzly bear

"Sounds like pretty good material for a book? You're right." — *The Boston Globe*

"Great fun to read." — *Daily News-Miner*, Fairbanks, Alaska

"Folks who use their bikes for more than trips to the corner store will love *Against the Wind*." — The *Union Leader*, Manchester, NH

Against the Wind is a light-hearted look at a most amazing journey. Follow along as Basch meets Jinkie Green, a cremated woman being carried to Alaska in a bicyclist's pannier. Follow the exploits of a few down-and-out cyclists in British Columbia, and find out how the Royal Canadian Mounted Police found the author's stolen bicycle helmet. Then, there's the author's incredible encounter with an Alaskan grizzly bear in Denali National Park.

Against the Wind is available directly from Top of the World Communications, PO Box 731, Intervale, NH 03845 for $12.95 plus $2.50 postage and handling. Or, pick it up at your local bookstore (ISBN 0-9646510-0-9). Sample pieces of *Against the Wind* at www.mountwashingtonvalley.com/top-of-the-world. Send e-mail to rodeman@aol.com.